AT MY TABLE
fresh and simple food

Artichokes.

AT MY TABLE
fresh and simple food

DONNA HAY
& QUENTIN BACON

A BARBARA BECKETT BOOK

A Barbara Beckett Book
First published in Australia in 1995 by
Barbara Beckett Publishing Pty Ltd
14 Hargrave Street, Paddington, Sydney, NSW 2021, Australia

Text copyright © Donna Hay 1995
Photographs copyright © Quentin Bacon and Donna Hay 1995
Production copyright © Barbara Beckett Publishing Pty Ltd 1995

This book is copyright.
Apart from any fair dealing for the purposes of private study, research, criticism or review, as permitted under the Copyright Act, no part may be reproduced by any process without written permission. Inquiries should be addressed to the publishers.

National Library of Australia
Cataloguing-in-Publication data:

    Hay, Donna.
    At my table: fresh and simple food.

    Includes index.
    ISBN 1 875891 03 X

    1. Cookery. I. Bacon, Quentin. II. Title.

641.5

Designed by Megan Smith and Barbara Beckett
Handwriting by Lachlan McPherson
Edited by Julia Cain
Index by Amanda Bilson

Printed in Hong Kong by
South China Printing Company (1988) Pty Limited

CONTENTS

Introduction 7

1 Summer fruits 11

2 Asparagus 27

3 Mushrooms 35

4 Capsicums, chilli peppers and tomatoes 43

5 Summer greens 59

6 Potatoes 71

7 Berry fruits 79

8 Garlic, onions and shallots 87

9 Winter vegetables 99

10 Eggplants 111

11 Herbs 119

12 Lemons, limes and tangelos 131

13 Winter fruits 143

14 Chocolate and coffee 151

15 The basics 167

Glossary 172

Index 174

Fresh from the market.

Introduction

ACKNOWLEDGEMENTS

A VERY BIG THANK YOU MUST GO TO . . .
all my family and friends for their support, encouragement and tolerance—to Lisa for being a great friend; Russell for keeping me laughing; Will and Ed for keeping me sane; Jody who is always reminding me to believe in myself, and who has been a wonderful work colleague from the very start; Lachlan McPherson for starting the ball rolling by allowing us to do an advertising campaign on polaroid transfer (yes, it's all your fault); Rachel Blackmore who took the chance and gave me my first major food styling job; Ben and Steph for the many cups of coffee and continuous studio organisation and help; Michael, David, Sam and Joe Antico for searching the markets for the almost impossible, finding all the perfect fruit and vegetables for this book; Bill Wilson my butcher; and Quentin, who worked on the book with me after we had both worked a full day, for giving up weekends, hours of sleep and socialising, and for constantly giving me a hard time whenever I am in the stucio (how silly it was of you to teach me how to punch properly).

PHOTOGRAPHY CREDITS
MISCELLANEA
napkins, cloths and crockery
trade enquiries
(02) 953 0123

DINOSAUR DESIGNS
Strand Arcade and Paddington,
Sydney.

THE BAY TREE KITCHEN SHOP
40 Holdsworth Street,
Woollahra, NSW 2025.

INTRODUCTION

My first memories of cooking are at the age of four, being with my grandmother, standing on a red chair at her stove, stirring a double boiler full of what was to be lemon curd. Once finished, my grandmother would let me eat it while it was still warm, spread on to fresh white bread. Then we would spoon it into jars and place them in the back of the refrigerator.

For me, great food is often connected with memorable occasions spent with friends and family. When I think of risotto and a simple rocket salad I immediately think of lunch in the studio with Quentin and Will. The same thing happens when I think of a cup of strong coffee and chocolate cake, immediately I think of my best friend Lisa. Vegetable curry is my sister Jo, cooking anything in a wok is Clayton and the two words healthy and vegetarian are truly my mum and dad.

Rarely do I conjure up a culinary masterpiece when I am eating alone, but there is nothing I like better than to create a feast for friends. When I cook I like to keep it simple with a mix of just a few flavours. The flavours can be complementary or contrasting—grilled limes for salmon or sugar-grilled figs with peppered crème fraîche. With some exceptions, such as an intricately spiced curry, I like food to be a few fresh and inspiring ingredients tossed together to create simple perfection. When food is laden with many flavours it is often a palate and senses battlefield, not unlike a group of frenzied buyers at a department store sale.

For those of you who are going to cook from this book I would like you to use my recipes as a starting point, to be changed to suit personal tastes or the cravings of the moment. When cooking for friends always remember these golden rules: don't drink too much before the guests arrive—and if your creative culinary skills have let you down, make sure the guests drink more than you do . . .
ENJOY

DONNA HAY

Summer fruits.

CHAPTER 1

Summer fruits

THAI BARBECUE PORK WITH APRICOT CHILLI SAMBAL

INGREDIENTS

1 kg (2 lbs) pork fillets

2 spring onions (scallions), chopped

2 teaspoons grated fresh ginger

1 fresh red chilli pepper, chopped

1 lemon grass stalk, chopped

2 tablespoons fresh coriander (cilantro) leaves

2 tablespoons lime juice

2 teaspoons ground cumin

1 tablespoon oil

Apricot Chilli Sambal

6 apricots

1 tablespoon palm sugar

2 fresh red chilli peppers

3 tablespoons coconut cream

1 tablespoon fresh coriander leaves

Trim the pork of any excess fat or sinew and set it aside. Place the spring onions, ginger, chilli pepper, lemon grass, coriander, lime juice, cumin and oil in a food processor or blender and process until a smooth paste has formed Spread the paste over the pork fillets, cover and refrigerate for 1 hour. Cook the pork on a preheated barbecue for 3 minutes each side or until it is cooked to your liking. Allow the pork to stand for 2 minutes before slicing.

To make apricot sambal, cut the apricots in half and remove the stones. Slice the apricots thinly, seed and chop the chilli peppers and place them in a bowl with the other ingredients. Cover and refrigerate for at least 2 hours to allow the flavours to develop.

To serve, place apricot chilli sambal on individual serving plates and top with slices of warm pork. Serve with rice noodles tossed with toasted sesame seeds.

SERVES 4

GRILLED SWORDFISH WITH NECTARINE SALSA

INGREDIENTS

1 kg (2 lbs) swordfish fillets

1 teaspoon pistachio oil

1 tablespoon olive oil

2 tablespoons lime juice

cracked black pepper

sea salt

2 tablespoons chopped lemon thyme

Nectarine Salsa

1 tablespoon yellow mustard seeds

3 tablespoons raspberry vinegar

4 nectarines

½ red onion, chopped

½ cup (60 g/2 oz) toasted pine nuts

60 g (2 oz) baby watercress, broken into small sprigs

To make nectarine salsa, place the mustard seeds and vinegar in a bowl and stand for 30 minutes. Cut the nectarines in half and remove the stones. Chop the nectarines into pieces and mix with the mustard seed mixture, red onion, pine nuts and watercress.

Brush the swordfish with the combined pistachio oil, olive oil and lime juice then toss the fish in the pepper, sea salt and thyme. Cook the swordfish under a preheated griller or broiler for 2–3 minutes each side or until cooked through (when the fish flakes).

To serve, place fish on individual serving plates with a pile of salsa and serve with kumera (sweet potato) chips (page 102).

SERVES 4

BALTI CHICKEN WITH GREEN MANGO SALSA

Heat the oil in a frying pan or skillet over a medium heat. Add the coriander seeds, cumin seeds, fennel seeds, mustard seeds, cardamom pod, cinnamon and curry leaves and cook for 2 minutes or until the seeds start to pop. Place the spice mixture and water into a small food processor and process until smooth, or pound the mixture using a mortar and pestle.

Return the spice mixture to the frying pan or skillet and add the chilli pepper, ginger and garlic and cook for 3 minutes. Add the chicken to the pan and cook for 3 minutes each side or until golden. Add the tomatoes and stock to the pan and simmer for 4–6 minutes or until the chicken is cooked through.

To make green mango salsa, peel and chop the mangoes, seed and chop the chilli peppers. Place all the ingredients in a bowl and mix well to combine. Stand for 30 minutes to allow the flavours to infuse before serving.

To serve, place the chicken on serving plates and top with pan juices. Serve with the salsa and jasmine rice.

SERVES 6

INGREDIENTS

1 tablespoon oil
1 tablespoon coriander seeds
1 tablespoon cumin seeds
1 teaspoon fennel seeds
1 teaspoon black mustard seeds
1 cardamom pod, bruised
1 teaspoon ground cinnamon
4 dried curry leaves
2 tablespoons water
1 fresh red chilli pepper, chopped
2 teaspoons grated fresh ginger
2 garlic cloves, crushed
6 chicken breast fillets
435 g (14 oz) can tomatoes, crushed
½ cup (125 mL/4 fl oz) chicken stock

Green Mango Salsa

2 green mangoes
2 tablespoons chopped fresh coriander (cilantro) leaves
2 fresh green chilli peppers
2 teaspoons grated lemon rind
2 tablespoons soft brown sugar
½ teaspoon ground cinnamon

PEACH, LEMON GRASS AND GINGER CHUTNEY

Heat the oil in a saucepan over a medium heat. Add the lemon grass, ginger, onions, chilli peppers and coriander and cook for 2 minutes, then reduce the heat to low.

Chop and remove the stones from the peaches and add to the saucepan with the vinegar, brown sugar and currants. Stir the mixture until the sugar has dissolved. Increase the temperature and simmer for 1½ hours, stirring occasionally, until the mixture is thick. Allow the chutney to cool and pour it into hot, sterilised jars. Seal and store in a dark, cool place. Refrigerate chutney after opening.

MAKES 5 CUPS

INGREDIENTS

2 teaspoons oil
3 lemon grass stalks, chopped
2 tablespoons grated fresh ginger
2 onions, chopped
2 fresh red chilli peppers, seeded and chopped
2 teaspoons ground coriander
1 kg (2 lbs) peaches, peeled
2 cups (500 mL/16 fl oz) white wine vinegar
1 cup (155 g/5 oz) soft brown sugar
¾ cup (125 g/4 oz) currants

OYSTERS WITH SALMON ROE AND PAWPAW

INGREDIENTS

2 tablespoons lime juice

1 tablespoon soft brown sugar

2 drops Tabasco or pepper sauce

½ small pawpaw (papaya)

24 large oysters in the shell

4 tablespoons salmon roe

chervil leaves

I use the large varieties of oyster for this recipe, such as bluff oysters or Jervis Bay oysters.

Mix together the lime juice, brown sugar and Tabasco sauce. Carefully peel and remove the seeds from the pawpaw then slice it into small, thin slices. Place a few pieces of pawpaw next to each oyster in its shell. Sprinkle with a little of the lime mixture and top with salmon roe and chervil leaves. Refrigerate until serving.

Serve as a first course with small pieces of toasted rye bread and glasses of well chilled champagne.

SERVES 4–6

TUNA AND NECTARINE BRUSCHETTAS

INGREDIENTS

12 slices crusty Italian bread

2 garlic cloves, halved

3 tablespoons olive oil

Dressing

2 teaspoons thinly sliced fresh ginger

1 tablespoon soy sauce

1 tablespoon mirin

2 teaspoons toasted sesame seeds

Topping

1 avocado, thinly sliced

2 nectarines, thinly sliced

2 tablespoons fresh coriander (cilantro) leaves

375 g (12 oz) tuna, sliced paper thin

Place the bread under a preheated griller or broiler and toast on both sides until golden. Rub the toasts with the garlic and brush with the olive oil.

To make dressing, combine the ingredients in a bowl and mix well.

To finish bruschettas, top the toasts with slices of avocado and nectarine and a few coriander leaves. Top with slices of tuna and drizzle with the dressing. Serve immediately with glasses of chilled, unoaked chardonnay.

SERVES 6 FOR DRINKS OR 4 AS A FIRST COURSE

Oysters with salmon roe and pawpaw and Tuna and nectarine bruschettas.

CHICKEN WITH PAWPAW AND WATERMELON SALSA

INGREDIENTS

4 chicken breast fillets
1 tablespoon ground paprika
2 teaspoons dried thyme leaves
1 teaspoon cracked black pepper
pinch chilli powder
2 teaspoons dried oregano leaves
olive oil

Pawpaw and Watermelon Salsa
½ small pawpaw (papaya), peeled and seeded
¼ small watermelon, seeds removed
3 spring onions (scallions), chopped
2 teaspoons grated lime rind
3 tablespoons pistachio nuts, roughly chopped
1 tomato, chopped
3 tablespoons sweet raspberry vinegar

Trim the chicken of any fat and make three slits across each fillet. Combine the paprika, thyme leaves, pepper, chilli powder and oregano leaves. Rub the chicken in the spice mixture and set aside. Place the chicken on a baking sheet, drizzle with the oil and place under a hot preheated griller (broiler) and cook for 2–3 minutes each side or until tender.

To make pawpaw and watermelon salsa, chop the pawpaw and watermelon into small chunks and place in a bowl with the spring onions, lime rind, pistachio nuts, tomato and raspberry vinegar. Mix well to combine, cover and refrigerate for 1 hour before serving.

To serve, place the chicken on serving plates and serve with generous spoonfuls of salsa.

SERVES 4

CHARRED SCALLOP SKEWERS

INGREDIENTS

500 g (16 oz) scallops (sea scallops)
2 mangoes, chopped into large chunks
2 red onions, cut into wedges

Marinade
2 tablespoons seeded mustard
2 teaspoons chopped fresh dill
2 tablespoons lemon juice
2 teaspoons honey
2 tablespoons oil
cracked black pepper

Thread the scallops, mango and onion onto metal skewers. Combine the marinade ingredients in a bowl and brush the mixture over the skewers. Place the skewers on a preheated hot barbecue or char-griller and cook for 1 minute each side or until browned and slightly charred. While cooking, continue to brush the skewers with the marinade.

Serve the scallop skewers with a salad of baby spinach, Parmesan cheese shavings, sun-dried capsicums and balsamic vinegar.

SERVES 4

CHAR-GRILLED MANGO WITH TOASTED COCONUT SALSA

Cut three slits in each mango half. Combine the lime juice, brown sugar, cinnamon and cardamom in a bowl and mix to combine. Brush well over the mangoes and place on a preheated char-griller and grill for 1 minute each side or until golden.

To make coconut salsa, place the coconut in a frying pan or skillet over a medium heat and cook, stirring, for 3 minutes or until golden. Add the sugar, lemon juice and pineapple and toss to combine. Cook for 1 minute then remove from the heat and stir in the mint leaves.

To serve, place the mango on individual serving plates and serve warm with coconut salsa and vanilla bean ice cream.

SERVES 6

INGREDIENTS

6 peeled mango halves
2 tablespoons lime juice
2 tablespoons soft brown sugar
1 teaspoon ground cinnamon
¼ teaspoon ground cardamom

Coconut Salsa
1 cup (90 g/3 oz) flaked coconut
3 tablespoons soft brown sugar, extra
1 tablespoon lemon juice
⅓ cup (75 g/2½ oz) finely chopped pineapple
1 tablespoon chopped fresh mint leaves

BALSAMIC WHITE PEACH SALAD

Halve the peaches and remove the stones then carefully cut the flesh into slices. Arrange the peach slices, cheese, rocket leaves and olives on individual serving plates. Sprinkle liberally with balsamic vinegar then give a light sprinkle of pepper and olive oil. Finish with a sprinkling of pepita seeds. Serve the salad as a first course or a light meal.

SERVES 6

INGREDIENTS

4 white peaches
350 g (11 oz) fresh farm curd or cottage cheese
250 g (8 oz) rocket (arugula) leaves
1⅔ cups (250 g/8 oz) niçoise olives
½ cup (125 mL/4 oz) balsamic vinegar
cracked black pepper
olive oil
125 g (4 oz) pepita (pumpkin) seeds, toasted

Poached peaches with mint anglaise and sugar grilled figs with peppered creme fraiche.

POACHED PEACHES WITH MINT ANGLAISE

Place the peaches in a bowl of boiling water and allow to stand for 6 minutes. Remove the peaches from the water and carefully peel away the skins. Put the sugar and water in a large saucepan over a low heat and stir until the sugar has dissolved. Add the vanilla bean and clove and increase the heat to a simmer. Add three peaches at a time and poach for 6–8 minutes or until the peaches are soft.

To make mint anglaise, place the milk, vanilla bean and mint in a saucepan and bring to the boil. Remove from the heat and allow to stand for 10 minutes so that the flavours infuse. Remove the vanilla bean and mint. Place the egg yolks and sugar in a bowl and beat until light and fluffy, then beat in the hot milk. Pour the mixture back into the saucepan over a low heat and stir for 6 minutes or until the custard coats the back of a wooden spoon.

To serve, place a peach in each serving bowl, accompanied by a dollop of mint anglaise and heavy (double) cream.

SERVES 6

INGREDIENTS

6 peaches

½ cup (125 g/4 oz) white granulated sugar

4 cups (1 litre/1¾ imp. pints) water

1 vanilla bean

1 clove

Mint Anglaise

2 cups (500 mL/16 fl oz) milk

1 vanilla bean, extra

2 mint sprigs

5 egg yolks

2 tablespoons white granulated sugar

SUGAR-GRILLED FIGS WITH PEPPERED CREME FRAICHE

Place the figs flesh side up on a baking sheet. Combine the brown sugar, butter and vanilla extract and spread the mixture over the cut side of the figs. Place them under a hot preheated griller (broiler) and cook for 2–3 minutes or until golden.

Combine the crème fraîche and the brandy and place a spoonful on each serving plate with the figs. Sprinkle the crème fraîche with the pepper and serve.

SERVES 6

INGREDIENTS

8 figs, halved

⅓ cup (60 g/2 oz) soft brown sugar

60 g (2 oz) butter, softened

1 teaspoon vanilla extract

Peppered Crème Fraîche

1 cup (250 mL/8 fl oz) crème fraîche

2 tablespoons brandy

2 teaspoons cracked black pepper

COCONUT ICE CREAM WITH MACERATED LYCHEES

INGREDIENTS

2 cups (185 g/6 oz) desiccated coconut, toasted

3 cups (750 mL/24 fl oz) light (single) cream

1 cup (250 mL/8 fl oz) milk

1 vanilla bean

6 egg yolks

½ cup (125 g/4 oz) caster (superfine) sugar

Macerated Lychees

350 g (11 oz) lychees, peeled

3 tablespoons orange juice

2 tablespoons Grand Marnier

3 tablespoons caster (superfine) sugar

1 cinnamon stick

1 bay leaf

Place the coconut, cream, milk and vanilla bean in a saucepan over a high heat and bring to the boil. Remove from the heat and allow to stand for 2 hours for the flavours to infuse. Strain the mixture through a sieve lined with muslin.

Place the egg yolks and caster sugar in a bowl and beat until light and creamy. Whisk in the cream mixture. Pour the mixture into a saucepan over a low heat and stir for 5 minutes or until the mixture has thickened slightly, cool.

Pour the mixture into an ice cream maker and follow manufacturer's instructions until the ice cream is thick and easily scooped out. Freeze until ready to serve.

To macerate lychees, remove seeds from lychees if you like and place the lychees in a bowl with the orange juice, Grand Marnier, caster sugar, cinnamon stick and bay leaf. Cover and refrigerate for at least 2 hours before serving. To serve, place the lychees in deep dessert plates and top with scoops of coconut ice cream.

SERVES 4–6

NECTARINE GRANITA

INGREDIENTS

1⅓ cups (340 g/11 oz) white granulated sugar

2 cups (500 mL/16 fl oz) water

8 nectarines

1 tablespoon grated orange rind

3 tablespoons tequila

Place the sugar and water in a saucepan over a low heat and stir until the sugar has dissolved. Increase the heat and bring the syrup to the boil. Allow to simmer for 4 minutes, then set aside to cool.

Remove the stones from the nectarines, place the flesh in a food processor or blender and process until smooth. Press the nectarine pulp through a sieve and place it in a bowl. Stir in the sugar syrup, orange rind and tequila.

Pour the mixture into a metal container and freeze it for 1 hour. Whisk a fork through the mixture to break up the ice crystals. Return to the freezer and freeze for 4 hours or until set. To serve, whisk a fork through the granita and spoon it into serving glasses.

SERVES 6

ICED VODKA BLOOD PLUM CREAM

Remove the stones from the plums and roughly chop the flesh. Place the plum flesh in a food processor or blender and process until smooth. Stir the plum liquid through a sieve. Place the plum purée and sugar in a saucepan over a low heat and stir until the sugar has dissolved. Allow the mixture to come to the boil then simmer for 4 minutes or until the mixture has thickened. Stir in the vodka and set aside to cool completely.

Place the cream in a large, chilled bowl and whip until soft peaks form. Stir in the orange rind and the plum purée. Oil six 1 cup (250 mL/8 fl oz) capacity dariole moulds and line them with plastic wrap (cling film). Pour the cream mixture into the moulds and place in the freezer. Freeze for 3 hours or until firm.

To make sautéed vodka plums, carefully cut the plums in half and remove the stones. Slice the plums into thick slices. Melt the butter in a frying pan or skillet over a high heat and allow to bubble. Add the brown sugar and stir until it has dissolved. Add plums, vodka and cinnamon to the pan and sauté for 1 minute or until heated through.

To serve, remove plum creams from moulds and place on chilled serving plates. Serve immediately with warm or room temperature sautéed vodka plums.

SERVES 6

INGREDIENTS

6 small plums

3 tablespoons white granulated sugar

1 tablespoon vodka

1¼ cups (310 mL/10 fl oz) heavy (double) cream

1 teaspoon finely grated orange rind

Sautéed Vodka Plums

4 blood plums

2 tablespoons butter

3 tablespoons soft brown sugar

3 tablespoons vodka

½ teaspoon ground cinnamon

ROSE GERANIUM AND MANGO ICE CREAM

Place the cream, milk and rose geranium leaves in a saucepan over a high heat and heat until almost boiling. Remove from the heat and set aside to cool. Place the egg yolks and sugar in a large bowl and beat until light and fluffy. Remove the rose geranium leaves from the cream mixture. Beat into the egg yolk mixture. Fold through the mango purée and pour into an ice cream maker. Follow the manufacturer's instructions until the ice cream is thick and frozen.

SERVES 8–10

INGREDIENTS

2 cups (500 mL/16 fl oz) light (single) cream

2 cups (500 mL/16 fl oz) milk

4 rose geranium leaves

9 egg yolks

1 cup (250 g/8 oz) white granulated sugar

2 cups (500 mL/16 fl oz) mango purée

VANILLA BRIOCHE WITH SLOW SIMMERED PLUMS

INGREDIENTS

½ cup (125 mL/4 fl oz) milk

1 vanilla bean, split

15 g (½ oz) dry yeast

3 cups (375 g/12 oz) plain (all-purpose) flour

⅓ cup (75 g/2½ oz) caster (superfine) sugar

2 eggs, lightly beaten

185 g (6 oz) butter, chopped

Simmered Plums

12 plums

½ cup (125 g/4 oz) white granulated sugar

2 cups (500 mL/16 fl oz) water

2 lemon rind pieces

2 mint sprigs

2 cassia bark (cinnamon) pieces

2 cloves

There is nothing quite like the smell of baking bread.

Pour the milk into a saucepan over a high heat, add the vanilla bean, and bring to the boil. Remove from the heat and allow to infuse until the milk is warm, then remove the vanilla bean. Add the yeast and a pinch of caster sugar to the milk and leave to stand until foaming.

Place the flour and caster sugar in a bowl and mix to combine. Add the eggs and the yeast mixture and mix to a smooth dough. Place the dough on a lightly floured surface and knead for 2 minutes. Add the butter a little at a time and knead well to combine until the dough is smooth.

Place the dough in a lightly oiled bowl, cover and stand in a warm place for 20 minutes or until the dough has doubled in size. Punch down the dough and knead it for 1 minute. Divide the dough into four equal pieces and shape into small loaves. Place in four greased 15 cm × 8 cm (6 in × 3 in) baby loaf tins, cover with a tea towel and leave to double in size. Bake in a preheated oven at 190°C (375°F) for 25–30 minutes or until golden and cooked through.

To make simmered plums, cut the plums in half and remove the stones. Place the sugar and water in a saucepan over a low heat and stir until the sugar has dissolved. Increase the heat and allow the syrup to boil for 5 minutes. Place the lemon rind, mint, cassia bark and cloves in a piece of muslin and tie it up. Place the muslin bag and plums in the saucepan and reduce the heat to a slow simmer. Allow the plums to very slowly simmer for 30–40 minutes or until very soft.

To serve, slice the brioche loaves into thick slices. Place the brioche slices under a medium preheated griller (broiler) and toast for 1 minute each side or until golden. Place on serving plates and serve immediately with the simmered plums and some heavy (double) cream.

SERVES 6

Vanilla brioche with slow simmered plums.

CHERRY CONFIT WITH HAZELNUT SHORTBREAD

INGREDIENTS

600 g (1¼ lbs) cherries

1 cup (250 mL/8 fl oz) light red wine

1⅓ cup (350 mL/11 fl oz) water

½ cup (125 g/4 oz) caster (superfine) sugar

1 vanilla bean

1 mint sprig

1 tablespoon orange rind strips

Spiced Cream

1 cup (250 mL/8 fl oz) heavy (double) cream

1 teaspoon freshly grated nutmeg

1 teaspoon finely grated fresh ginger

½ teaspoon ground cinnamon

2 teaspoons icing (confectioners')sugar

Hazelnut Shortbread

155 g (5 oz) butter

1 teaspoon vanilla extract

¼ cup (45 g/1½ oz) soft brown sugar

1 cup (125 g/4 oz) plain (all-purpose) flour

½ cup (60 g/2 oz) ground hazelnuts

Remove the stems from the cherries and prick each cherry a few times with a pin. Place the red wine, water, caster sugar, vanilla bean, mint and orange rind in a large saucepan over a low heat and stir until the sugar has dissolved.

Increase the heat and allow the mixture to boil for 4 minutes. Reduce the heat to a simmer and add the cherries to the pan. Simmer slowly for 30 minutes or until the cherries are very soft and the liquid is syrupy. Remove the vanilla bean and mint.

To make spiced cream, place the ingredients in a bowl and fold together to combine. Refrigerate until required.

To make hazelnut shortbread, place the butter, vanilla extract and brown sugar in a bowl and beat until light and creamy. Stir in the flour and hazelnuts and mix well to combine. Place tablespoons of the mixture on greased baking sheets. Bake in a preheated oven at 180°C (355°F) for 12 minutes or until golden. Allow the shortbread to cool on the baking sheets.

To serve, place spoonfuls of warm or cold cherry confit in deep dessert bowls, accompanied by a spoonful of spiced cream and a hazelnut shortbread.

SERVES 6

MELON AND CHAMPAGNE SORBET

INGREDIENTS

1 cup (250 mL/8 fl oz) champagne

1 cup (250 g/8 oz) white granulated sugar

2 cups (500 mL/16 fl oz) watermelon purée

2 cups (500 mL/16 fl oz) honeydew or rockmelon purée

2 tablespoons lime juice

Place the champagne and sugar in a saucepan over a low heat and stir until the sugar has dissolved. Increase the temperature and allow the mixture to simmer for 1 minute. Transfer the champagne mixture to a bowl, add the watermelon and honeydew melon purées and mix well.

Pour the mixture into an ice cream maker and follow the manufacturer's instructions until the sorbet is firm. Freeze until ready to serve. To serve, place scoops of sorbet with fresh fruits in glass dishes. Serve with a glass of champagne.

SERVES 4–6

NECTARINES WITH MAPLE ICE CREAM

Carefully cut the nectarines in half and remove the stones. Place the nectarines on a greased baking sheet, sprinkle with brandy then set aside. Place the demerara sugar, lime juice, coconut and sour cream in a bowl and mix to combine. Pile the mixture on top of the nectarine halves. Bake the nectarines in a preheated oven at 180°C (355°F) for 20 minutes or until the topping is golden and the nectarines are soft.

To make maple ice cream, place the cream and vanilla bean in a saucepan over a medium heat. Allow the cream to almost boil, remove from heat, cool for 5 minutes, then remove the vanilla bean.

Place the egg yolks in a bowl and beat until light and creamy. Gradually add the maple syrup and beat well. Whisk the cream into the egg yolk mixture and continue whisking until combined. Pour the mixture into a saucepan over a low heat and stir constantly until the mixture has thickened slightly (about 6 minutes).

Allow the mixture to cool, and then place in an ice cream maker and freeze according to manufacturer's instructions. To serve, place warm nectarines onto serving plates and add generous scoops of maple ice cream. Pour pan juices over the nectarines before serving.

SERVES 6

INGREDIENTS

6 nectarines

⅓ cup (90 mL/3 fl oz) brandy

⅓ cup (60 g/3 oz) demerara sugar

2 tablespoons lime juice

1 cup (45 g/1½ oz) shredded coconut

3 tablespoons sour cream

Maple Ice Cream

4 cups (1 litre/1¾ imp. pints) light (single) cream

1 vanilla bean

8 egg yolks

1 cup (250 mL/8 fl oz) maple syrup

PEACH CREME FRAICHE CAKE

Place the butter and maple syrup in a frying pan or skillet over a medium heat and cook at a simmer, stirring, for 5 minutes. Add the peaches and cook for 3 minutes or until soft. Place the peaches in the bottom of a well-greased 23 cm (9½ in) round cake tin and pour over the maple syrup. Set aside. Place the butter, caster sugar and orange rind in a bowl and beat until light and creamy. Gradually add the eggs and beat well. Fold in the crème fraîche, poppy seeds and flour.

Spoon the mixture over the peaches in the cake tin. Bake in a preheated oven at 180°C (355°F) for 35–40 minutes or until the cake is cooked when tested with a skewer. Allow the cake to stand for 5 minutes before inverting it onto a serving plate.

To serve, cut the warm cake into wedges and serve with sweetened mascarpone or heavy (double) cream.

SERVES 8–10

INGREDIENTS

60 g (2 oz) butter

⅓ cup (90 mL/3 fl oz) maple syrup

4 peaches, peeled and halved

125 g (4 oz) butter

⅔ cup (155 g/5 oz) caster (superfine) sugar

1 tablespoon grated orange rind

2 eggs

⅔ cup (185 mL/6 fl oz) crème fraîche

3 tablespoons poppy seeds

1½ cups (185 g/6 oz) self-raising flour

Asparagus.

CHAPTER 2

Asparagus

BASIL AND ASPARAGUS SOUP

INGREDIENTS

2 teaspoons oil

2 garlic cloves, crushed

2 potatoes, peeled and chopped

750 g (1½ lbs) asparagus

4 cups (1 litre/1¾ imp. pints) chicken or vegetable stock

1 cup (250 mL/8 fl oz) light (single) cream

3 tablespoons chopped young fresh basil leaves

8 slices crusty bread

250 g (8 oz) Brie, sliced

8 cherry tomatoes, halved

cracked black pepper

Heat the oil in a saucepan over a medium heat. Add the garlic and sauté for 2 minutes or until golden. Add the potatoes and cook, stirring, for 3 minutes. Chop the asparagus and set the tips aside. Add the asparagus stalks and stock to the saucepan and simmer for 10 minutes.

Place the mixture in a food processor or blender and process until smooth. If the asparagus is stringy, stir the mixture through a sieve and then return it to the saucepan. Add the cream, basil and asparagus tips and simmer for 4 minutes.

Place the bread slices on a baking sheet and brush with oil. Top with the Brie, tomatoes and pepper and bake in a preheated oven at 180°C (355°F) for 12–15 minutes or until the bread and cheese are golden.

To serve, ladle the soup into deep, warmed bowls and serve with Brie toasts on the side.

SERVES 4–6

ASPARAGUS TIED WITH CRISP PROSCIUTTO

INGREDIENTS

24 asparagus spears

8 slices prosciutto (Parma) ham

60 g (2 oz) butter, chopped

1 tablespoon lemon juice

cracked black pepper

4 slices toasted rye bread

Place the asparagus in four bundles of 6 spears each. Tie the prosciutto around the bundles at the tops and bases. Place in a baking pan, dot with butter and sprinkle with lemon juice and pepper.

Bake in a preheated oven at 180°C (355°F) for 15–20 minutes or until the asparagus is tender and the prosciutto is crisp.

To serve, place asparagus bundles on toasted rye bread and serve with small mounds of whole egg mayonnaise (page 169), seeded mustard and tomato jam.

SERVES 4

CHAR-GRILLED ASPARAGUS WITH BALSAMIC

Wash, dry and trim off the thick asparagus ends. Brush the asparagus with the olive oil and place on a very hot char-grill plate. Cook for 4 minutes or until tender. Place the asparagus on a warm serving plate.

To make balsamic dressing, place the vinegar, oil, mustard and pepper in a bowl and mix to combine. Pour the dressing over the warm asparagus and garnish with Parmesan cheese shavings.

SERVES 4

INGREDIENTS

500 g (1 lb) asparagus
1 tablespoon olive oil

Balsamic Dressing
3 tablespoons balsamic vinegar
2 tablespoons macadamia nut oil
1 tablespoon grainy mustard
ground black pepper

ASPARAGUS, COUS COUS AND WARM HUMMUS DRESSING

To make hummus dressing, place the chickpeas, tahini, garlic, cumin, coriander, chilli sauce and ricotta cheese in a food processor or blender and process until smooth. Add enough vegetable stock to make a mayonnaise consistency.

Place the cous cous in a bowl and set aside. Heat the vegetable stock in a small saucepan until boiling and pour over the cous cous. Cover and stand for 5 minutes or until the stock has been absorbed. Separate the grains with a fork. Heat the oil in a frying pan or skillet over a high heat. Add the garlic, onion, mustard seeds and chilli pepper and sauté for 4 minutes or until the onions are golden and the mustard seeds start to pop. Trim the ends from the asparagus and slice them in half. Add them to the frying pan with the zucchini and wine and sauté for 3–4 minutes or until the asparagus is tender.

To serve, gently warm the hummus dressing in a saucepan over a low heat. Pile spoonfuls of cous cous on serving plates, top with the asparagus mixture and pour over the warm hummus dressing. Serve with warm flat breads, olives and feta cheese.

SERVES 4

INGREDIENTS

1¼ cups (250 g/8 oz) cous cous
1½ cups (375 mL/12 fl oz) vegetable stock
2 teaspoons oil
2 garlic cloves, crushed
1 onion, sliced
1 tablespoon black mustard seeds
1 fresh green chilli pepper, seeded and chopped
500 g (1 lb) asparagus
2 baby zucchini (courgettes), sliced
3 tablespoons dry white wine

Warm Hummus Dressing
1 cup (170 g/5½ oz) cooked or canned chickpeas (garbanzo beans)
3 tablespoons tahini
2 garlic cloves, crushed
1 teaspoon ground cumin
1 tablespoon chopped fresh coriander (cilantro) leaves
1 tablespoon sweet chilli sauce
250 g (8 oz) ricotta cheese
⅓ cup (90 mL/3 fl oz) vegetable stock

Chargrilled asparagus with balsamic.

TAMARIND PRAWNS WITH CARAMELISED ASPARAGUS

Place the oils in a wok, frying pan or skillet over a high heat. Add the lemon grass, garlic, coriander, chillies and tamarind paste and sauté for 4 minutes. Add the palm sugar, lime juice and prawns and sauté for 5 minutes or until the prawns are bright and cooked through.

To caramelise asparagus, melt the butter in a frying pan or skillet over a medium heat. Allow the butter to foam and then add the brown sugar, stirring well. Add the asparagus and cook, tossing in the butter, for 5 minutes or until tender. Stir in the lemon rind.

To serve, place the asparagus on serving plates and top with tamarind prawns. Serve with jasmine rice and sweet chilli sauce.

SERVES 4–6

INGREDIENTS

2 teaspoons peanut oil

1 teaspoon sesame oil

1 lemon grass stalk, finely chopped

2 garlic cloves, crushed

5 coriander (cilantro) roots, chopped

2 fresh green chilli peppers, seeded and chopped

2 teaspoons tamarind paste

2 tablespoons palm sugar

2 tablespoons lime juice

750 g (1½ lbs) large green prawns (shrimps), peeled

Caramelised Asparagus

60 g (2 oz) butter

2 tablespoons soft brown sugar

500 g (1 lb) asparagus, trimmed and halved

1 teaspoon grated lemon rind

ASPARAGUS WITH POPPYSEED VINAIGRETTE

To make vinaigrette, place the ingredients in a bowl and whisk to combine.

Trim the ends from the asparagus and plunge the spears into boiling water for 15–20 seconds or until they have turned bright green. Place in a shallow dish, pour over the vinaigrette and allow to stand for at least 30 minutes.

To serve, place asparagus on a bed of baby spinach leaves and top with the macadamia nuts and the vinaigrette remaining in the dish.

SERVES 4–6

INGREDIENTS

750 g (1½ lbs) asparagus

225 g (7 oz) baby spinach leaves

½ cup (30 g/1 oz) toasted macadamia nuts

Poppyseed Vinaigrette

2 tablespoons poppyseeds

⅓ cup (90 mL/3 fl oz) orange juice

2 teaspoons Dijon mustard

⅓ cup (90 mL/3 fl oz) macadamia nut oil

3 tablespoons red wine vinegar

2 teaspoons honey

SMOKED CHICKEN AND GRILLED STRACCHINO SANDWICHES

Brush the bread slices with the olive oil and place them under a preheated hot griller (broiler). Grill until golden brown on both sides.

Cut the chicken into paper thin slices and place them on the toasted bread. Trim the asparagus and cut the spears in half. Plunge them into a saucepan of boiling water and then rinse under cold water. Top the chicken with the asparagus and a squeeze of lemon.

Top the sandwiches with the tomatoes, basil leaves and stracchino cheese and sprinkle with pepper. Place under a preheated hot griller for 1 minute or until the stracchino is melted and golden. Serve immediately with a glass of red wine.

SERVES 4

INGREDIENTS

8 slices crusty sour dough or Italian bread
olive oil

Topping
4 smoked chicken breast fillets
375 g (12 oz) asparagus
lemon juice
2 egg-shaped (Roma/plum) tomatoes, thinly sliced
fresh basil leaves
340 g (11 oz) stracchino cheese, sliced
cracked black pepper

ASPARAGUS TEMPURA WITH ASIAN MAYONNAISE

To make Asian mayonnaise, place the ingredients in a bowl and mix to combine. Cover and refrigerate until required.

To make tempura batter, place the flour in a bowl and make a well in the centre. Add the water, egg yolks and enough mineral water to make a smooth, thin batter the consistency of cream.

Trim the ends from the asparagus and heat a saucepan of oil over a high heat. Dip the asparagus into the batter and then place in the hot oil. Allow to cook for 1 minute or until slightly browned and crisp. Place on absorbent kitchen paper to drain and serve hot with small ramekins of Asian mayonnaise to dip the asparagus into.

SERVES 4–6

INGREDIENTS

750 g (1½ lbs) asparagus
vegetable oil for deep frying

Tempura Batter
2¼ cups (280 g/9 oz) plain (all-purpose) flour
2 cups (500 mL/16 fl oz) iced water
2 egg yolks
1 cup (250 mL/8 fl oz) carbonated mineral water, well chilled

Asian Mayonnaise
¾ cup whole egg mayonnaise (page 169)
3 tablespoons tamari
2 teaspoons chopped preserved pink ginger
2 tablespoons sake
1 teaspoon sesame oil

Mushrooms.

CHAPTER 3

Mushrooms

WINE, BEEF AND MUSHROOM PIES

INGREDIENTS

750 g (1½ lbs) ready-made puff pastry

1 egg yolk

pinch salt

Filling

2 teaspoons oil

2 onions, chopped

500 g (1 lb) lean blade steak, cubed

1½ cups (375 mL/12 fl oz) rich beef stock

½ cup (125 mL/4 fl oz) tomato purée (passata)

1 cup (250 mL/8 fl oz) red wine

375 g (12 oz) champignon (button) mushrooms, halved

1 tablespoon Worcestershire sauce

1 tablespoon chopped fresh sage leaves

cracked black pepper

To make filling, heat the oil in a frying pan or skillet over a medium heat, add the onions and cook for 4 minutes or until they are well browned. Add the beef to the pan and cook for 5 minutes or until it is well browned. Add the stock, tomato purée and red wine to the pan and reduce the heat to a simmer. Allow the mixture to simmer for 35 minutes then add the mushrooms and Worcestershire sauce and simmer for a further 10–15 minutes, or until the beef is tender. Stir in the sage leaves and pepper to taste. Remove from the heat and allow to cool while you are lining the tins with pastry.

Roll out the pastry on a lightly floured surface until 4 mm (⅙ in) thick. Line the bases of six 2 cm (5 in) pie tins with pastry and pour in the cooled filling. Use the remaining pastry to cover the pies, seal and make a few steam holes with a fork. Mix the egg yolk with the salt and brush it over the pastry tops.

Bake the pies in a preheated oven at 180°C (355°F) for 25–30 minutes or until the pastry is puffed and golden. Serve with mashed potatoes and a good homemade chutney (page 52).

SERVES 6

FIELD MUSHROOM PIZZAS

INGREDIENTS

1 quantity pizza dough (page 170)

1 tablespoon olive oil

⅓ cup (60 g/2 oz) cornmeal (polenta)

Topping

1 tablespoon butter

1 red onion, chopped

2 teaspoons green peppercorns, lightly crushed

8 large field mushrooms, sliced

2 tablespoons chopped garlic chives

⅓ cup (45 g/1½ oz) pecan nuts, chopped

90 g (3 oz) Gorgonzola, crumbled

90 g (3 oz) provolone, grated

Place the pizza dough on a lightly floured surface and press down with the palm of your hand to flatten it slightly. Place the oil and cornmeal in the middle of the dough and knead well to combine. Divide the dough into four equal portions and roll into rounds about 4 mm (⅙ in) thick. Place on greased baking sheets and set aside.

To make topping, melt the butter in a frying pan or skillet over a high heat. Add the onion and cook for 2 minutes or until soft. Add the peppercorns and mushrooms and cook for 3 minutes or until the mushrooms are soft.

Divide the mushroom mixture between the dough bases and sprinkle with garlic chives, pecan nuts, Gorgonzola and provolone. Bake in a preheated oven at 200°C (390°F) for 25–30 minutes or until the base is golden and crisp. Serve with balsamic marinated tomatoes and baby endive (frisée).

SERVES 4

WOK MUSHROOMS WITH SOBA NOODLES

Heat the chilli oil in a wok over a high heat. Add the spring onions and ginger and cook for 1 minute. Add the prawns and stir-fry for 4 minutes or until they have changed colour and browned slightly then remove them from the wok and set aside.

Add the shoyu, sake and brown sugar to the wok and cook, stirring, for 3 minutes or until the liquid is reduced by half. Add the mushrooms and snow peas and cook for 2–3 minutes or until soft. Return the prawns to the pan and cook for 1–2 minutes or until they are heated through.

To cook soba noodles, place them in a saucepan of boiling water for 3–5 minutes or until just tender, drain well. Toss them in a bowl with the sesame seeds, chilli pepper and coriander leaves.

To serve, place piles of soba noodles on serving plates and top with the prawn and mushroom mixture. Serve warm with steamed greens and small glasses of warm sake.

SERVES 4

INGREDIENTS

2 teaspoons chilli oil

4 spring onions (scallions), sliced

2 teaspoons fresh grated ginger

500 g (1 lb) green prawns (shrimp), peeled

⅓ cup (90 mL/3 fl oz) shoyu

⅓ cup (90 mL/3 fl oz) sake

1 tablespoon soft brown sugar

375 g (12 oz) mixed mushrooms (enokitake, shiitake, swiss brown)

185 g (6 oz) snow peas (mangetout), trimmed and sliced

Soba Noodles

250 g (8 oz) green soba noodles

3 tablespoons toasted sesame seeds

1 fresh red chilli pepper, seeded and chopped

1 tablespoon fresh coriander (cilantro) leaves

MUSHROOM AND GOLDEN ONION TART

To make topping, melt the butter in a frying pan or skillet over a low heat. Add the onions and cook, stirring occasionally, for 10 minutes or until they are golden and soft. Add the thyme, vinegar and mushrooms and cook for 3 minutes.

Roll out the pastry on a lightly floured surface to form a 30 cm × 20 cm (12 in × 8 in) rectangle. Top with the onion and mushroom filling, leaving a 2 cm (¾ in) border. Place on an oiled baking sheet and bake in a preheated oven at 180°C (355°F) for 25 minutes or until the pastry is puffed and golden.

SERVES 6

INGREDIENTS

280 g (9 oz) ready-made puff pastry

Topping

60 g (2 oz) butter

4 medium onions, sliced

2 tablespoons fresh chopped thyme leaves

2 tablespoons balsamic vinegar

340 g (11 oz) champignon (button) mushrooms, halved

155 g (5 oz) oyster mushrooms

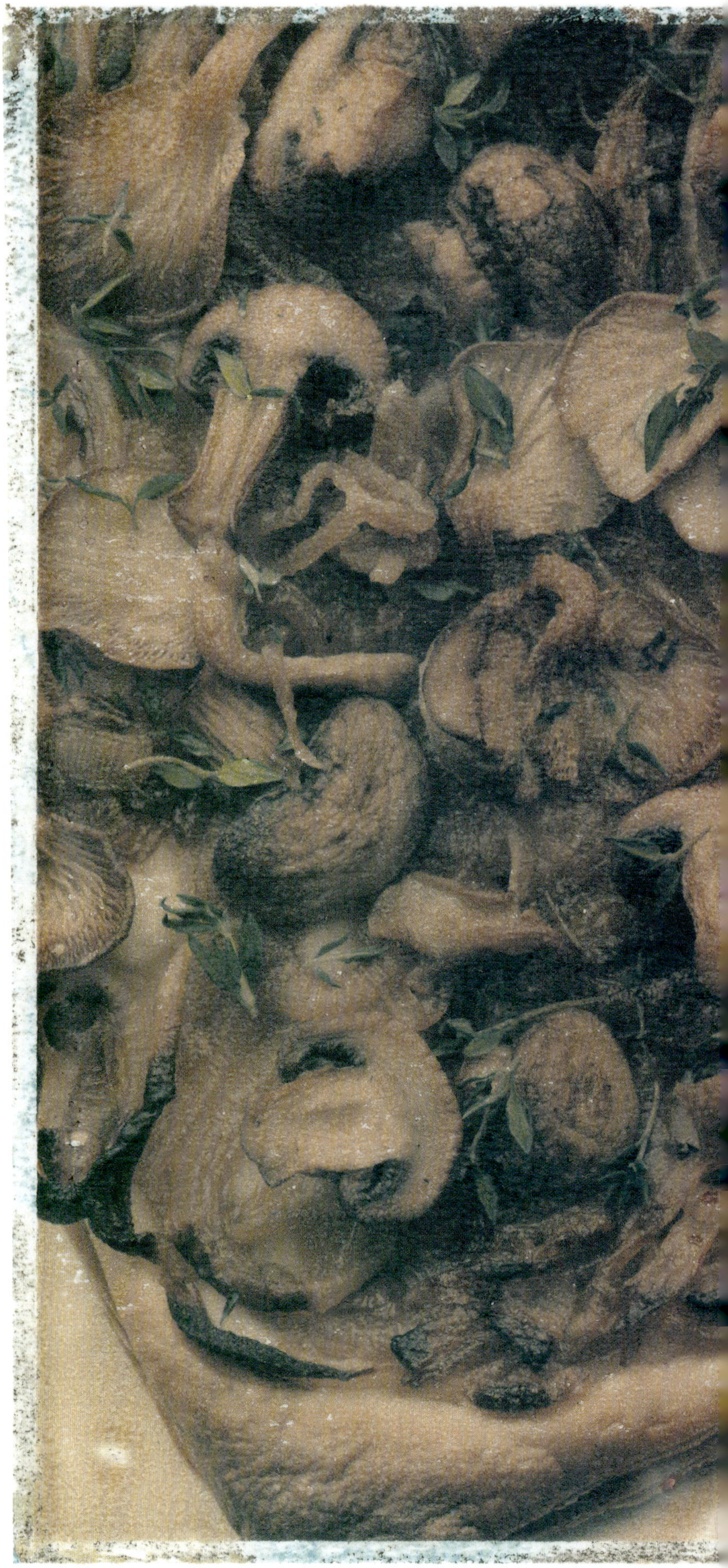

Mushroom and golden onion tart.

MUSHROOM LASAGNE

INGREDIENTS

vegetable oil for deep frying

12 wonton wrappers

Champignon Layer

2 teaspoons oil

1 garlic clove, crushed

250 g (8 oz) champignon (button) mushrooms, halved

3 tablespoons vegetable stock

3 tablespoons dry white wine

½ teaspoon grated lemon rind

3 tablespoons crème fraîche

cracked black pepper to season

Oyster Mushroom Layer

2 teaspoons oil

2 spring onions (scallions), chopped

250 g (8 oz) oyster mushrooms

3 tablespoons beef stock

1 vine-ripened tomato, chopped

2 bocconcini, chopped

1 tablespoon fresh basil leaves, chopped

To make champignon layer, heat the oil in a frying pan or skillet over a medium heat and add garlic. Sauté for 1 minute or until the garlic is golden. Add the mushrooms and sauté for 4 minutes or until they turn golden then add the stock, wine and lemon rind and simmer for 5 minutes or until the mushrooms are soft and the liquid has reduced. Stir in the crème fraîche and pepper, then set aside and keep warm. To make oyster mushroom layer, heat the oil in a frying pan or skillet over a medium heat. Add the spring onions and cook for 1 minute, then add the oyster mushrooms and sauté for 2 minutes. Pour in the beef stock, add the tomato and simmer for 3 minutes or until the tomato has softened slightly and the liquid has reduced. Stir in the bocconcini and basil leaves and keep warm.

Heat the deep frying oil until hot then place the wonton wrappers, a few at a time, in the hot oil and fry until golden (1–2 minutes). Remove from oil using a slotted spoon and set aside to drain on absorbent kitchen paper. Repeat the process with all the wontons.

To serve, place crisp wontons on four serving plates. Top the wontons with the champignon mixture and top with another wonton wrapper. To finish, top with oyster mushroom mixture and the remaining wontons. Serve with a salad of greens.

SERVES 4

PESTO FIELD MUSHROOMS

INGREDIENTS

12 large field mushrooms

1 cup (200 g/6½ oz) cous cous

1½ cups (375 mL/12 fl oz) boiling water

1 cup pesto (page 169)

90 g (3 oz) sun-dried capsicums, chopped

2 spring onions (scallions), chopped

1 tablespoon baby capers, rinsed

155 g (5 oz) marinated feta cheese, roughly chopped

60 g (2 oz) butter, melted

cracked black pepper

Remove the stalks from the mushrooms, place them on greased baking sheets and set aside. Place the cous cous in a bowl, pour over the boiling water, cover and stand for 5 minutes. Spread the insides of the mushroom caps with the pesto. Stir the cous cous with a fork to break up the grains, add the sun-dried capsicums, onions, capers and feta cheese and toss to combine. Fill the mushrooms with the cous cous mixture and pour a little of the melted butter over each of the mushrooms. Top with a sprinkling of pepper, and bake in preheated oven at 180°C (355°F) for 30 minutes or until the mushrooms are soft. To serve, arrange the mushrooms on serving plates and serve with chunks of warm baguette (French bread stick).

SERVES 4

CHAMPAGNE MUSHROOM RISOTTO

William, this recipe is for you so I never have to handwrite this recipe for you again.

Melt the butter in a saucepan over a medium heat until foaming. Add the garlic and mushrooms and sauté for 4 minutes or until golden. Add the thyme leaves and champagne and simmer for 3 minutes or until the mushrooms are soft. Remove the mushrooms from the pan and set aside.

Add the extra butter to the saucepan and melt over a medium heat until foaming. Add the rice and cook, stirring, for 4 minutes or until the grains are translucent. In another saucepan, heat the stock, champagne and saffron threads over a medium heat and allow the liquid to come to the boil. Reduce the temperature and keep this liquid hot.

Add 1 cup of the stock mixture to the rice and stir until the liquid has been absorbed. Repeat this process, 1 cup of liquid at a time, until all the liquid has been absorbed and the rice is creamy and soft. Add the mushroom mixture, snow peas and Parmesan cheese to the saucepan and stir for 3 minutes or until heated through.

To serve, spoon the risotto into deep bowls and top with a generous sprinkling of pepper and Parmesan cheese shavings.

SERVES 4–6

INGREDIENTS

1 tablespoon butter

1 garlic clove, crushed

310 g (10 oz) mixed mushrooms of your choice

1 tablespoon fresh chopped thyme leaves

⅓ cup (90 mL/3 fl oz) champagne

2 tablespoons butter, extra

2 cups (435 g/14 oz) Arborio rice

2 cups (500 mL/16 fl oz) vegetable stock

2 cups (500 mL/16 fl oz) champagne

3 saffron threads

155 g (5 oz) snow peas (mangetout), trimmed and halved

⅓ cup (45 g/1½ oz) grated Parmesan cheese

cracked black pepper

Parmesan cheese shavings

DRIED MUSHROOM OIL

This oil makes a great base for for stir-fries, Asian foods or for any foods where a subtle, spiced, Asian mushroom oil will enhance the flavour.

Place the oil in a saucepan and heat over a low heat until warm. Add the star anise pod, mushrooms, galangal, garlic and chilli peppers. Remove from the heat and allow to stand until cool.

Pour the oil into sterilised jars and seal. Store in the refrigerator after opening. The oil should keep for approximately 3 months.

MAKES 2¼ CUPS

INGREDIENTS

2 cups (500 mL/16 fl oz) vegetable oil

1 star anise pod

8 dried Chinese mushrooms

4 slices galangal or 4 slices fresh ginger

2 garlic cloves, halved

2 fresh red chilli peppers, halved

Capsicums, chilli peppers and tomatoes.

CHAPTER 4

Capsicums, chilli peppers and tomatoes

ROASTED CAPSICUM SOUP WITH CHILLI SCONES

INGREDIENTS

2 teaspoons oil

1 red onion, chopped

4 tomatoes, peeled, seeded and chopped

4 red capsicums (sweet peppers), halved and roasted (page 170)

2 cups (500 mL/16 fl oz) vegetable stock

1 tablespoon chopped fresh basil leaves

1 tablespoon chopped fresh mint leaves

cracked black pepper

Chilli Scones

2 cups (250 g/8 oz) self-raising flour

30 g (1 oz) butter

2 fresh red chilli peppers, seeded and chopped

1 teaspoon ground cumin

1 tablespoon chopped fresh coriander (cilantro) leaves

1 cup (250 mL/8 fl oz) milk

To make soup, heat the oil in a saucepan over a medium heat. Add the onions and sauté for 3 minutes or until soft. Add the tomatoes and cook for a further 5 minutes or until soft. Place the onion mixture in a food processor or blender with the capsicums and 1 cup of vegetable stock and process until smooth. Transfer the mixture back to the saucepan with the remaining stock and cook for 5 minutes or until well heated through. Stir in the basil and mint leaves and pepper.

To make chilli scones, place the flour in a bowl and with cool fingertips rub in the butter. Add the chilli peppers, cumin and coriander leaves to the flour mixture and mix well. Add enough milk to form a soft, sticky dough. Place the dough on a lightly floured surface and press out until it is 2 cm ($^2/_3$ in)thick.

Cut the scones into 5 cm (2 in) rounds and place on a greased baking sheet about 1 cm ($^1/_3$ in) apart. Bake in a preheated oven at 230°C (450°F) for 15 minutes or until puffed and golden.

To serve, ladle the soup into warmed serving bowls and top with a swirl of mascarpone. Serve with warm chilli scones on the side.

SERVES 4–6

FREE FORM ROAST CAPSICUM PIES

Divide the pastry into four equal portions and roll out on a lightly floured surface into 4 mm (⅙ in) thick circular shapes.

To make filling, place the capsicums, thyme leaves, feta cheese and basil leaves in a bowl and toss to combine. Divide the filling between the pastry rounds and pile in the middle of each pastry.

Fold in the pastry edges to form a rim and pinch them at the base so that the pastry stands upright. Place on a greased baking sheet and refrigerate for 30 minutes or until the pastry is firm.

Bake in a preheated oven at 200°C (390°F) for 25 minutes or until the pastry is golden and crisp.

To serve, place the pies on serving plates and drizzle with balsamic vinegar. Serve with sweet onion marmalade (page 89) and rocket (arugula) leaves.

SERVES 4

INGREDIENTS

1 quantity shortcrust pastry (page 168)

Filling

2 red capsicums (sweet peppers), roasted and sliced (page 170)

2 yellow capsicums (sweet peppers), roasted and sliced (page 170)

2 green capsicums (sweet peppers), roasted and sliced (page 170)

1 tablespoon fresh thyme leaves

280 g (9 oz) feta cheese, crumbled

2 tablespoons fresh basil leaves

2 tablespoons balsamic vinegar

BAKED ANTIPASTO PEPPERS

Cut the capsicums lengthwise and remove the seeds. Place the capsicums on baking sheets. Place the tomatoes, artichokes, olives, feta cheese, mushrooms and oregano leaves in a bowl and toss to combine.

Spoon the mixture into the capsicums, drizzle with the olive oil and vinegar and sprinkle with the pepper. Bake in a preheated oven at 190°C (375°F) for 30 minutes or until the capsicums are soft and the filling is hot.

To serve, place on serving plates and serve with barbecued meat skewers and warm flat bread.

SERVES 6

INGREDIENTS

3 red capsicums (sweet peppers)

Filling

6 egg-shaped (Roma/plum) tomatoes, halved

6 artichoke hearts, halved

¾ cup (125 g/4 oz) black olives

250 g (8 oz) marinated feta cheese, chopped

12 champignon (button) mushrooms, quartered

1 tablespoon fresh oregano leaves

2 tablespoons olive oil

2 tablespoons red wine vinegar

cracked black pepper

Chilli jam.

CHILLI JAM

Heat the oil in a large frying pan or skillet over a high heat. Add the mustard seeds, cumin and coriander seeds and cook for 3 minutes or until the seeds start to pop. Add the onions, garlic and chilli peppers and cook for a further 4 minutes or until the onions are golden.

Place the onion and spice mixture in a food processor or blender and process until finely chopped. Return the mixture to the saucepan and add the tomatoes, brown sugar, vinegar and water. Cook over a low heat for 1½ hours or until the mixture has thickened. When cool, spoon the mixture into sterilised jars and seal. The jam should keep for approximately 3 months.

MAKES 3 CUPS

INGREDIENTS

3 tablespoons oil

2 tablespoons black mustard seeds

1 tablespoon cumin seeds

1 tablespoon coriander seeds

2 onions chopped

3 garlic cloves, crushed

5 fresh red chilli peppers, chopped

8 large tomatoes, peeled, seeded and chopped

3 tablespoons soft brown sugar

3 tablespoons malt vinegar

1 cup (250 mL/8 fl oz) water

ROAST TOMATO AND MINT PESTO TART

Roll out the pastry on a lightly floured surface until 4 mm (⅙ in) thick. Cut the pastry into a 30 cm × 20 cm (12 in × 8 in) rectangle. Use leftover pastry to form a border by cutting it into 1 cm (⅓ in) wide strips and placing them around the edges of the pastry. Place the pastry on a lined or greased baking sheet.

To make mint pesto, place the mint and basil leaves, pine nuts, Parmesan cheese and garlic in a food processor or blender and process until finely chopped. Add the oil and process well. Pesto should be fairly dry. Spread the pesto over the pastry and refrigerate until required.

Place the tomatoes on a greased baking sheet and sprinkle generously with the oil and pepper. Bake the tomatoes in a preheated oven at 150°C (300°F) for 1 hour or until they are very soft. Place the tomatoes on top of the pesto-topped pastry and bake at 200°C (390°F) for 20 minutes or until the pastry is golden and puffed.

To serve, cut the tart into wedges and serve with a cress salad. This tart can be served warm or cold.

SERVES 6

INGREDIENTS

375 g (12 oz) ready-made puff pastry

Mint Pesto

¾ cup (30 g/1 oz) fresh mint leaves

¾ cup (30 g/1 oz)) fresh basil leaves

⅓ cup (45 g/1½ oz) pine nuts

½ cup (60 g/2 oz) grated Parmesan cheese

2 garlic cloves, crushed

2 tablespoons olive oil

Tomato Topping

8 egg-shaped (Roma/plum) tomatoes, halved

2 tablespoons olive oil, extra

cracked black pepper

RATATOUILLE AND PARMESAN CHEESE TARTS

INGREDIENTS

1 quantity shortcrust pastry (page 168)

Filling

1 small eggplant (aubergine), chopped

sea salt

2 teaspoons oil

2 onions, chopped

1 garlic clove, crushed

1 red capsicum (sweet pepper), chopped

1 green capsicum (sweet pepper), chopped

2 small zucchinis (courgettes), chopped

4 tomatoes, peeled and chopped

2 tablespoons tomato paste (purée)

½ cup (125 mL/4 fl oz) red wine

½ cup (125 mL/4 fl oz) vegetable stock

2 tablespoons chopped fresh parsley

1 tablespoon chopped fresh basil leaves

cracked black pepper

½ cup (60 g/2 oz) grated Parmesan cheese

Roll out the pastry on a lightly floured surface until 4 mm (⅙ in) thick. Line four 12 cm (5 in) removable base tart tins with pastry, trim the edges and prick the bases with a fork. Line the tart shells with baking parchment and fill with baking weights or rice. Bake in a preheated oven at 180°C (355°F) for 8 minutes. Remove the weights and paper and return to the oven for 4–5 minutes or until the pastry is golden.

To make filling, place the eggplant in a colander and sprinkle with sea salt. Allow to drain for 10 minutes then rinse well. Heat the oil in a large frying pan or skillet over a high heat. Add the onion and garlic and sauté for 4 minutes or until golden. Add the eggplant, red and green capsicums, zucchini, tomatoes, tomato paste, red wine and stock and bring to the boil. Reduce the heat and allow the mixture to simmer for 15 minutes or until the vegetables are soft.

Stir in the parsley, basil leaves and pepper and spoon the filling into the tart shells. Top with the Parmesan cheese and place in the oven for 10 minutes or until the Parmesan cheese has melted and the tarts are heated through.

SERVES 4

CHILLI AND PEPPER OIL

INGREDIENTS

6 small fresh red chilli peppers, halved

1½ cups (375 mL/12 fl oz) olive oil

2 teaspoons black peppercorns, lightly smashed

2 pieces lime rind

Place the ingredients in a saucepan over a low heat and heat gently for 10 minutes. Remove from the heat and set aside to cool.

Strain the oil mixture through muslin, pour it into sterilised bottles and seal. Store in a dark, cool cupboard and refrigerate after opening. The oil should keep for approximately 12 months.

MAKES 1½ CUPS (375ML/12 FL OZ)

TANDOORI BAKED VEGETABLES

Amazing flavours develop when these vegetables are allowed to marinate for a good few hours.

Heat the oil in a frying pan or skillet over a high heat, add the onion, garlic and ginger and cook for 3 minutes or until the onion is soft. Add the cumin, chilli peppers, coriander, paprika and cardamom and cook for a further 2 minutes.

Place the onion and spice mixture, lemon rind, lemon juice, yoghurt and fresh coriander in a food processor or blender and process until smooth.

Place the tandoori mixture in a large bowl. Add the potatoes, corn and sweet potato and toss to coat. Allow to stand for 2 hours. Remove the vegetables from the tandoori mixture and place on a greased wire rack that has been placed in a baking pan. Brush the vegetables with any remaining tandoori mixture then bake in a preheated oven at 200°C (390°F) for 35–45 minutes or until the vegetables are tender and golden.

Serve the tandoori vegetables with lime wedges and warm naan bread or with grilled baby lamb cutlets.

SERVES 4–6

INGREDIENTS

1 tablespoon oil

1 onion, chopped

2 garlic cloves, crushed

2 teaspoons grated fresh ginger

2 teaspoons ground cumin

2 fresh red chilli peppers, seeded and chopped

2 teaspoons ground coriander

1 tablespoon paprika

1 teaspoon ground cardamom

2 teaspoons grated lemon rind

2 tablespoons lemon juice

½ cup (90 g/3 oz) plain yoghurt

2 tablespoons chopped fresh coriander (cilantro) leaves

375 g (12 oz) baby potatoes

2 corn cobs, cut into 8 cm (3 in) pieces

375 g (12 oz) sweet potato, peeled and sliced thickly

THAI SALAD WITH CHILLI COCONUT DRESSING

Arrange the chicken, snow pea sprouts, tomatoes, and bok choy on a serving plate. Sprinkle with basil and refrigerate until required.

To make dressing, seed and chop the chilli peppers. Combine the chilli peppers, coconut milk, lime juice and sesame oil. Pour the dressing over the salad before serving. Serve the salad with thin slices of toasted pumpkin bread.

SERVES 4

INGREDIENTS

4 chicken breasts, cooked and sliced

125 g (4 oz) snow pea (mangetout) sprouts

250 g (8 oz) yellow tear drop tomatoes, halved

250 g (8 oz) baby bok choy, separated

2 tablespoons fresh Thai basil leaves

Chilli Coconut Dressing

2 fresh red chilli peppers

½ cup (125 mL/4 fl oz) coconut milk

2 tablespoons lime juice

2 teaspoons sesame oil

CHILLI NOODLE CAKES WITH TAPENADE

INGREDIENTS

1 Chinese barbecued duck, warm

Chilli Noodle Cakes

225 g (7 oz) rice noodles

2 fresh red chilli peppers, chopped

2 nori sheets, toasted and shredded

oil for shallow frying

Capsicum Tapénade

2 red capsicums (sweet peppers), roasted and peeled

¾ cup (125 g/4 oz) pitted black olives, chopped

2 teaspoons chilli oil

1 tablespoon pomegranate molasses or balsamic vinegar

To make capsicum tapénade, place the ingredients in a bowl and mix to combine. Cover and place in the refrigerator for at least 30 minutes to allow the flavours to develop.

To make chilli noodle cakes, place the rice noodles in a bowl and cover with boiling water. Allow to stand for 5 minutes or until the noodles are soft then drain them well and place on absorbent kitchen paper to dry. Place the noodles in a bowl and mix in the chilli peppers and nori.

Heat the oil in a frying pan or skillet over a medium heat and place spoonfuls of the noodle mixture in the pan. Cook for 2 minutes each side or until golden brown

To serve, cut the duck flesh away from the bones and slice into small pieces. Top the noodle cakes with the duck and with the capsicum tapénade. Serve as a light meal or as a first course.

SERVES 4–6

COUS COUS WITH ROAST TOMATOES AND BROTH

INGREDIENTS

1½ cups (310 g/10 oz) cous cous

1½ cups (375 mL/12 fl oz) boiling water

Roast Tomatoes

8 egg-shaped (Roma/plum) tomatoes, halved

1 tablespoon olive oil

cracked black pepper

2 oregano sprigs

Saffron Broth

2 teaspoons oil

2 garlic cloves, sliced

2 spring onions (scallions), chopped

½ teaspoon saffron threads

1⅓ cups (340 mL/11 fl oz) vegetable stock

3 tablespoons dry white wine

To roast tomatoes, place the tomatoes on a baking sheet and sprinkle with the olive oil, pepper and oregano. Bake in a preheated oven at 120°C (245°F) for 2 hours or until soft and pulpy. Keep warm.

Place the cous cous in a bowl and pour over the boiling water. Cover and allow to stand for 5 minutes or until the water is absorbed. Stir with a fork to break up the grains, cover and keep warm.

To make saffron broth, heat the oil in a saucepan over a medium heat and add the garlic and spring onions. Sauté for 3 minutes or until golden. Add the saffron threads, stock and wine and simmer for 5 minutes.

To serve, place piles of cous cous on serving plates. Carefully spoon the saffron broth over the cous cous and top with the roast tomatoes. Serve with thinly sliced, rare roast lamb.

SERVES 4

Chilli noodle cakes with tapenade.

EGGPLANT, TOMATO AND MUSTARD SEED CHUTNEY

INGREDIENTS

1 kg (2 lbs) eggplants (aubergines), chopped

sea salt

2 tablespoons olive oil

2 onions, sliced

2 tablespoons black mustard seeds

1 tablespoon cumin seeds

3 fresh red chilli peppers, chopped

1 teaspoon turmeric

500 g (1 lb) tomatoes, peeled, seeded and chopped

1 cup (250 mL/8 fl oz) tomato purée (passata)

2½ cups (625 mL/1 imp. pint) malt vinegar

1¼ cups (200 g/6½ oz) soft brown sugar

This chutney is great to serve with curries or on open sandwiches or hamburgers.

Place the eggplants in a colander, sprinkle with the sea salt and allow to drain for 10 minutes. Rinse thoroughly, drain and pat dry with absorbent kitchen paper. Heat the oil in a large saucepan over a medium heat. Add the onions, mustard seeds, cumin seeds, chilli peppers and turmeric and cook, stirring, for 5 minutes or until the seeds start to pop and the onion turns golden.

Add the eggplant and cook for 5 minutes or until the eggplant has browned slightly. Add the tomatoes, tomato purée, vinegar and brown sugar to the pan and stir over a low heat until the sugar has dissolved. Bring the mixture to the boil then reduce the heat and allow it to simmer for 45 minutes or until the mixture has thickened. Pour into hot sterilised jars and seal when the mixture is cold. Store in a cool, dark cupboard and refrigerate after opening. The chutney should keep for approximately 6 months.

MAKES 5 CUPS

FRAGRANT GREEN CHICKEN CURRY

Seed and chop the chilli peppers. Place the coriander leaves, chilli peppers, cumin seeds, ginger, spring onions, garlic, cardamom, lime juice, curry leaves and cinnamon in a food processor or blender and process to a smooth paste. Heat the oil in a frying pan or skillet over a medium heat, add the curry paste and cook, stirring, for 3 minutes. Add the chicken and cook for 4 minutes or until the chicken is golden brown. Add the stock and coconut milk and allow to simmer, uncovered, for 10 minutes or until the chicken is tender.

To make mango sambal, place the ingredients in a bowl and toss to combine.

To serve, stir in the Kaffir lime leaves and place on serving plates. Serve with mango sambal and fried lentils or jasmine rice.

SERVES 4

INGREDIENTS

3 fresh long green chilli peppers
2 tablespoons chopped fresh coriander (cilantro) leaves
2 teaspoons cumin seeds
2 teaspoons chopped fresh ginger
4 spring onions (scallions), chopped
1 garlic clove, crushed
½ teaspoon ground cardamom
2 tablespoons lime juice
4 fresh or dried curry leaves
½ teaspoon ground cinnamon
1 tablespoon oil
6 chicken thigh fillets, halved
1 cup (250 mL/8 fl oz) chicken stock
1 cup (250 mL/8 fl oz) coconut milk
2 Kaffir lime leaves

Mango Sambal
1 banana, chopped
1 mango, chopped
2 tablespoons lemon juice
3 tablespoons toasted coconut
3 tablespoons cashew nuts, chopped

FRIED LEEK COUS COUS WITH HARISSA

To make harissa, remove the stems and seeds from the chilli peppers and place in a bowl. Cover with boiling water and allow to stand for 15 minutes or until the chilli peppers are very soft. Drain the chilli peppers and place in a food processor or blender with the coriander seeds, cumin seeds, garlic and sea salt and process until very finely chopped. While the motor is running, gradually add the oil and process to a smooth paste. Cool and store in a sterilised jar in the refrigerator. The harissa should keep for approximately 6 months.

To make leek cous cous, place the cous cous in a bowl and pour over the boiling water. Cover and allow to stand for 5 minutes. Use a fork to separate the grains and set aside.

Heat the oil in a frying pan or skillet over a medium heat. Add the leeks and sauté for 6 minutes or until well browned. Add the cous cous, pine nuts and harissa and toss to combine. Cook for 1 minute or until heated through. Serve with lavash bread, harissa and char-grilled lamb loin.

SERVES 6 MAKES ¾ CUP HARISSA

INGREDIENTS

Harissa
1 cup (60 g/2 oz) dried chilli peppers
2 tablespoons coriander seeds
1½ tablespoons cumin seeds
3 garlic cloves, crushed
1 tablespoon sea salt
2 tablespoons olive oil

Cous cous
2 cups (405 g/13 oz) cous cous
2½ cups (625 mL/20 fl oz) boiling water
1 tablespoon oil
3 leeks, sliced
⅓ cup (45 g/1½ oz) pine nuts, toasted

GREEN TOMATO PANINI

INGREDIENTS

4 small rounds of soft focaccia bread

Filling

1 tablespoon olive oil

3 green tomatoes, thickly sliced

8 slices coppa or prosciutto (Parma) ham

4 bocconcini, sliced thickly

2 teaspoons fresh thyme leaves

cracked black pepper

2 teaspoons baby capers, rinsed

To make filling, heat the oil in a frying pan or skillet over a medium heat. Place the tomatoes in the pan and cook for 1 minute each side or until the tomatoes have softened slightly.

Place the coppa and bocconcini on bases of bread and top with the tomato slices. Sprinkle with the thyme leaves and pepper. Top with capers and bread tops. Place on a baking sheet in a preheated oven at 180°C (355°F) for 15 minutes or until well heated. Serve immediately with rocket (arugula) and baby endive (frisée) greens.

SERVES 4

LEMON AND CHILLI OLIVES

INGREDIENTS

1 kg (2 lbs) brined olives

rind from 2 lemons

4 fresh red chilli peppers, sliced

4 bay leaves

3 garlic cloves, sliced

3 rosemary sprigs, roughly chopped

olive oil

Drain the olives and place them in a large bowl. Cover with water and stand for 1 hour. Drain the olives, cover with fresh water and let stand for a further hour, then drain. Slice lemon rind into thin strips.

Add the lemon rind, chilli peppers, bay leaves, garlic and rosemary to the olives and toss to combine. Pack the olives into sterilised jars and pour over enough olive oil to cover. Seal and place on a sunny window sill for 2 to 3 days, then store in a dark, cool cupboard. Once opened, store in the refrigerator.

KEEPS FOR UP TO 4 MONTHS

Green tomato Panini and Lemon and chilli olives.

CHILLI BLACK-EYED BEANS WITH CORNBREAD

INGREDIENTS

Chilli Beans

1¼ cups (250 g/8 oz) black-eyed beans

2 teaspoons oil

2 onions, chopped

2 small fresh red chilli peppers, seeded and chopped

1 teaspoon cumin seeds

1 green capsicum (sweet pepper), chopped

1 red capsicum (sweet pepper), chopped

6 tomatoes, peeled, seeded and chopped

2 tablespoons tomato paste (purée)

½ cup (125 mL/4 fl oz) red wine

1½ cups (375 mL/12 fl oz) beef stock

375 g (12 oz) smoked ham bones

Cornbread

4 bacon rashers (slices)

1 cup (185 g/6 oz) cornmeal (polenta)

1 cup (125 g/4 oz) self-raising flour

½ teaspoon baking powder

2 tablespoons white granulated sugar

1 egg

1 cup (250 mL/8 fl oz) buttermilk

75 g (2½ oz) butter, melted

1 teaspoon good chilli powder

½ teaspoon ground cumin

2 jalapeño chilli peppers, chopped

To make cornbread, cook the bacon under a hot preheated griller (broiler) for 2 minutes each side or until golden and crisp. Break into small pieces and set aside. Place the cornmeal, flour, baking powder and sugar in a bowl and mix to combine. Add the egg, buttermilk, butter, chilli powder, cumin, chilli peppers and bacon and mix well to combine.

Pour the mixture into a greased 23 cm (9 in) round cake tin and bake in a preheated oven at 220°C (425°F) for 30 minutes or until the bread is golden and cooked through.

To make chilli beans, place the black-eyed beans in a bowl and cover with boiling water. Allow to stand for 4 hours or overnight. Drain and place in a saucepan with enough water to generously cover the beans. Allow the beans to boil for 30 minutes or until almost tender, then drain.

Heat the oil in a large saucepan over a medium heat. Add the onion, chilli peppers and cumin seeds and cook for 3 minutes or until the onion is golden. Add the capsicums, tomatoes, tomato paste, red wine, stock and ham bones and simmer for 15 minutes.

Add the black-eyed beans and simmer for a further 20 minutes or until the beans are soft. Remove the ham bones, chop the ham from the bones and return the meat to the mixture.

To serve, place the chilli beans in bowls and serve with slices of warm cornbread.

SERVES 4–6

CAPSICUM, ROCKET AND OLIVE PIZZETTAS

Divide the pizza dough into eight equal portions and roll out on a lightly floured surface until 4 mm (⅙ in) thick. Place on greased baking sheets and set aside.

To make topping, place the olives, basil leaves and sun-dried tomatoes in a food processor or blender and process until the mixture is a smooth, thick paste. Spread over the pizza bases leaving a 1 cm (⅓ in) border. Top with the rocket leaves and slices of red and yellow capsicums. Add the Parmesan shavings and bake in a preheated oven at 200°C (390°F) for 20 minutes or until the bases are golden. Serve with a marinated tomato salad.

SERVES 8 AS A SNACK OR 4 AS A MEAL

INGREDIENTS

1 quantity pizza dough (page 170)

Topping
¾ cup (125 g /4 oz) pitted black olives
3 tablespoons fresh basil leaves
4 sun-dried tomatoes
185 g (6 oz) rocket (arugula) leaves
2 red capsicums (sweet peppers), roasted (page 170)
2 yellow capsicum (sweet peppers), roasted (page 170)
½ cup (60 g/2 oz) Parmesan cheese shavings

LIME AND CHILLI ICE CREAM

Place the lime juice and sugar in a saucepan over a low heat and stir until the sugar has dissolved. Add the chilli peppers and increase the heat to bring the mixture to a simmer. Simmer the syrup for 3 minutes. Allow to cool slightly.

Beat the egg yolks in a bowl until thick and creamy. Add the sugar syrup in a slow stream and beat well.

Place the milk, cream, lime rind and vanilla bean in a saucepan over a medium heat and heat until almost boiling. Allow to stand for 6 minutes before removing the vanilla bean and lime rind. Pour the milk mixture into the egg mixture and beat well. Pour into a saucepan and stir over a low heat until the mixture thickens slightly and coats the back of a wooden spoon.

Allow the mixture to cool before pouring it into an ice cream maker. Follow the manufacturer's instructions until the ice cream is thick and scoopable. Place in a metal container and freeze until required. Serve with slices of fresh mango.

SERVES 6

INGREDIENTS

½ cup (125 mL/4 fl oz) lime juice
1 cup (250 g/8 oz) white granulated sugar
3 small fresh red chilli peppers, seeded and chopped
8 egg yolks
1½ cups (375 mL/12 fl oz) milk
1 cup (250 mL/8 fl oz) light (single) cream
rind from 2 limes
1 vanilla bean

Summer Greens.

CHAPTER 5

Summer greens

MIZUNA WITH PEACHES AND RASPBERRY VINAIGRETTE

INGREDIENTS

310 g (10 oz) mizuna

3 peaches, sliced

6 bocconcini, halved

8 slices prosciutto (Parma) ham

Raspberry Vinaigrette

225 g (7 oz) raspberries

3 tablespoons white wine vinegar

1 tablespoon white granulated sugar

1 tablespoon olive oil

2 teaspoons chopped fresh mint leaves

1 tablespoon chopped fresh chives

cracked black pepper

To make raspberry vinaigrette, place the raspberries in a food processor or blender and process until smooth. Stir the raspberries through a sieve and mix the purée with the vinegar, sugar, oil, mint leaves, chives and pepper.

Arrange the mizuna, peaches, bocconcini and prosciutto on serving plates, sprinkle with raspberry vinaigrette and serve with crusty bread.

SERVES 4

COS WITH CODDLED EGG DRESSING

INGREDIENTS

1 cos (romaine) lettuce

8 slices air-dried beef

60 g (2 oz) sun-dried capsicums (sweet peppers), chopped

Coddled Egg Dressing

2 eggs

4 tablespoons olive oil

1 tablespoon white wine vinegar

1 garlic clove, crushed

3 tablespoons grated pecorino cheese

1 tablespoon chopped fresh basil leaves

cracked black pepper

Break the cos into separate leaves, wash well and dry. Arrange the cos leaves, beef and capsicums on serving plates.

To make dressing, place the eggs in a saucepan of boiling water and cook for 1 minute. Place under cold water to cool. Peel the eggs, place in a bowl and whisk them well. Gradually add the remaining ingredients, whisking to combine. Pour the dressing over the cos leaves and serve with toasted rye bread.

SERVES 4

BEET GREENS WITH CAESAR DRESSING

Choose the small beet greens and they are delicious raw.

Arrange the beet greens on a serving plate. Spread the pesto over the baguette slices and place on a baking sheet. Bake in a preheated oven at 180°C (355°F) for 15 minutes or until crisp. Allow to cool. Place baguette slices, tomatoes and Parmesan cheese on the beet greens and toss to combine.

To make dressing, place all the ingredients in a bowl and mix to combine. Pour over the beet greens and serve.

SERVES 4

INGREDIENTS

310 g (10 oz) beet greens

½ cup ready-made pesto (page 169)

16 slices baguette (French bread stick)

125 g (4 oz) cherry tomatoes, halved

125 g (4 oz) Parmesan cheese shavings

Caesar Dressing

⅓ cup whole egg mayonnaise (page 169)

2 tablespoons white wine vinegar

2 tablespoons water

1 tablespoon seeded mustard

3 anchovies, rinsed and chopped

OAK LEAF SALAD NICOISE

Heat the oil in a frying pan or skillet over a high heat. Cut the tuna into 4 cm (1½ in) thick slices and rub the tuna with the peppercorns. Place in the pan and cook for 30 seconds each side or until well seared.

Wash and pat dry the lettuce leaves. Arrange the green and red oak leaf lettuce leaves on serving plates and top with the olives. Slice the eggs and add them to the salad with the onions.

To make dressing, place all the ingredients in a bowl and mix to combine. Place the tuna on top of the salad and pour over the dressing.

SERVES 4

INGREDIENTS

2 teaspoons oil

375 g (12 oz) fresh tuna

1 tablespoon green peppercorns, crushed

1 green oak leaf lettuce

1 red oak leaf lettuce

⅓ cup (60 g/2 oz) marinated olives

3 eggs, boiled until still soft

1 red onion, sliced

Dressing

2 tablespoons olive oil

2 tablespoons lemon juice

1 tablespoon chopped fresh parsley

2 teaspoons hot mustard

Scallop and nasturtium salad and Endive and white fig salad.

SCALLOP AND NASTURTIUM SALAD

Peppery nasturtiums with lightly spiced scallops.

Melt the butter in a frying pan or skillet over a medium heat and cook until foaming. Add the garlic, lime juice and ginger and cook for 3 minutes. Add the scallops and toss them in the butter mixture for 2 minutes or until cooked through. Keep warm.

Arrange the nasturtium leaves and flowers, cucumber and pistachio nuts on serving plates. Top with the warm scallops and sprinkle with the dressing.

To make dressing, place the ingredients in a bowl and mix to combine.

SERVES 4

INGREDIENTS

1 tablespoon butter
2 garlic cloves, crushed
2 tablespoons lime juice
2 teaspoons chopped pickled ginger
500 g (1 lb) scallops (sea scallops)
340g (11 oz) small nasturtium leaves and flowers
1 small cucumber, cut into thin strips
⅓ cup (45 g/1½ oz) pistachio nuts

Dressing
3 tablespoons mirin
1 tablespoon tamari
2 teaspoons sesame oil
1 tablespoon toasted sesame seeds

ENDIVE AND WHITE FIG SALAD

A simple yet perfect salad.

Divide the endives into four small bunches and tie them up with the chives. Place on a serving plate with a wedge of cheddar or Parmesan cheese and the figs.

To make dressing, press the raspberries through a sieve. Mix with the balsamic vinegar, sprinkle with pepper and pour over the endives and figs.

SERVES 4

INGREDIENTS

185 g (6 oz) baby endives (frisée)
4 chives
185 g (6 oz) aged cheddar or Parmesan cheese
8 small white figs, quartered

Raspberry Dressing
225 g (7 oz) raspberries
2 tablespoons balsamic vinegar
cracked black pepper

SORREL AND SALMON WITH LEMON DRESSING

INGREDIENTS

340 g (11 oz) small sorrel leaves
125 g (4 oz) lamb's lettuce (corn salad)
1 cucumber, cut into long thin strips
375 g (12 oz) smoked salmon slices

Lemon Dressing
3 tablespoons lemon juice
2 teaspoons chopped fresh mint leaves
2 teaspoons chopped fresh dill leaves
2 tablespoons oil
2 teaspoons honey

Wash, dry and arrange the sorrel and lamb's lettuce on individual serving plates. Top with small piles of cucumber and smoked salmon.

To make dressing, place all the ingredients in a bowl and whisk to combine. Drizzle the dressing over the salad just before serving. Serve with a selection of breads.

SERVES 4

BAKED RADICCHIO AND HALOUMI BRUSCHETTAS

INGREDIENTS

8 slices Italian bread
olive oil
1 garlic clove, halved

Topping
8 thin slices Black Forest smoked ham
8 radicchio leaves
8 thick slices haloumi
herbed oil
cumin seeds

Brush the bread with the olive oil and place on a baking sheet. Bake in a preheated oven at 180°C (355°F) for 10 minutes or until golden. Remove from the oven and rub the bruschettas with the cut garlic clove.

Top bruschettas with the ham, radicchio and haloumi. Sprinkle with herbed oil and a few cumin seeds. Return to the oven and bake for 15 minutes or until the haloumi is warm and golden.

Serve bruschettas warm with a glass of red wine and a bowl of warm, marinated olives.

SERVES 4

ROCKET AND FARM CHEESE SANDWICHES

Remove the crusts from the bread and place four pieces of bread on a board. Top the bread with rocket leaves then mix together the mayonnaise and balsamic vinegar and sprinkle it over the rocket. Top with Parmesan cheese and tomatoes and another slice of bread.

Top the bread with farm cheese and sprinkle with pepper, olives and basil leaves. Top with the remaining bread slices, cut into small triangles and serve with minted iced tea.

SERVES 4

INGREDIENTS

12 slices soft white bread

Rocket Filling

125 g (4 oz) rocket (arugula) leaves

⅓ cup whole egg mayonnaise (page 169)

2 tablespoons balsamic vinegar

⅓ cup (45 g/1½ oz) grated Parmesan cheese, sliced

2 egg-shaped (Roma/plum) tomatoes, sliced

Farm Cheese Filling

250 g (8 oz) farm cheese or fresh curd cheese, sliced

cracked black pepper

⅓ cup 60 g (2 oz) pitted olives, chopped

fresh basil leaves

WATERCRESS PESTO

A peppery pesto that is great with almost anything.

Place the watercress leaves, Parmesan cheese, macadamia nuts and garlic in a food processor or blender and process until finely chopped. Gradually add the oil while the motor is running and process to a smooth paste.

Use watercress pesto on pasta, in triple-layer soft, white bread sandwiches with fresh mozzarella cheese and vine tomatoes or spoon it on baked potatoes with sour cream.

MAKES 1 CUP

INGREDIENTS

1½ cups (60 g/2 oz) watercress leaves

⅓ cup (45 g/1½ oz) grated Parmesan cheese

⅓ cup (30 g/1 oz) roasted macadamia nuts

1 garlic clove, crushed

3 tablespoons olive oil

BABY COS AND MARINATED TUNA

INGREDIENTS

1 head baby cos (Romaine) lettuce

Marinated Tuna
375 g (12 oz) sashimi tuna
1 tablespoon grated fresh ginger
2 tablespoons sake
3 tablespoons soy sauce
2 teaspoons chilli oil
1 tablespoon lemon juice

These next two recipes are dedicated to Will and Edwina's parties.

To marinate tuna, slice the tuna very thinly with a sharp knife. Place the ginger, sake, soy sauce, chilli oil and lemon juice in a bowl and mix to combine. Pour over the tuna and allow to marinate for 15 minutes.

Wash and dry the baby cos leaves and arrange on serving plates. Top with the marinated tuna and serve with rice wafers.

SERVES 4

PASTA WITH ROCKET SAUCE

INGREDIENTS

500 g (1 lb) angel hair pasta

Rocket Sauce
2 teaspoons olive oil
2 garlic cloves, crushed
2 onions, sliced
1 tablespoon lemon juice
3 tablespoons white wine
2 teaspoons soft brown sugar
225 g (7 oz) rocket (arugula) leaves
cracked black pepper
pecorino cheese shavings

Place the angel hair pasta in a saucepan of boiling water and cook over a medium heat for 8 minutes or until tender. Drain.

While the pasta is cooking, heat the oil in a frying pan or skillet over a medium heat. Add the garlic and onions and sauté for 4 minutes or until golden. Add the lemon juice, wine and brown sugar and cook for 3 minutes. Toss the rocket through the onion mixture and then toss this mixture through the hot angel hair pasta.

Serve in deep pasta bowls topped generously with pepper and pecorino cheese shavings, and with slices of toasted walnut bread.

SERVES 4

Baby cos and marinated tuna.

EGG NOODLES WITH CHINESE BROCCOLI

INGREDIENTS

1 teaspoon sesame oil

2 teaspoons peanut oil

4 spring onions (scallions), chopped

1 tablespoon grated fresh ginger

2 tablespoons sweet chilli sauce

2 tablespoons hoisin sauce

2 tablespoons oyster sauce

2 teaspoons tamarind paste

375 g (12 oz) Chinese broccoli, chopped into large pieces

125 g (4 oz) snow peas (mangetout), trimmed and sliced

435 g (14 oz) fresh egg noodles

½ cup (75 g/2½ oz) roasted unsalted peanuts

Heat the oils in a wok over a high heat. Add the spring onions and cook for 1 minute. Add the ginger, sweet chilli sauce, hoisin sauce, oyster sauce and tamarind paste and cook for 2 minutes. Add the broccoli and snow peas and toss them in the sauce for 3 minutes. Keep warm.

Place the egg noodles in a saucepan of boiling water and cook for 3 minutes or until just tender. Drain and add to the wok, tossing together with the broccoli mixture.

Sprinkle with peanuts and serve with slices of barbecued Chinese duck or barbecued pork.

SERVES 4–6

CRESS AND STILTON PASTRIES

INGREDIENTS

375 g (12 oz) ready-made puff pastry

Filling

2 teaspoons oil

6 spring onions (scallions), chopped

4 bacon rashers (slices), chopped

2 eggs, lightly beaten

⅓ cup (90 g/3 oz) sour cream

1 cup (45 g/1½ oz) watercress leaves

225 g (7 oz) Stilton cheese, crumbled

⅓ cup (45 g/1½ oz) pine nuts

Perfect for Sunday lunch.

Roll out the pastry on a lightly floured surface until it is 4 mm (⅙ in) thick. Line six 12 cm (5 in) tart tins with pastry and trim the edges.

To make filling, heat the oil in a frying pan or skillet over a medium heat. Add the spring onions and the bacon and cook for 5 minutes or until the bacon is crisp. Allow the mixture to cool slightly.

Place the eggs, sour cream, watercress leaves and Stilton cheese in a bowl and mix to combine. Add the bacon mixture to the egg mixture and pour into pastry shells. Sprinkle with pine nuts and bake in a preheated oven at 200°C (390°F) for 20 minutes or until the pastry is golden and puffed and the filling is set.

SERVES 6

SAUTEED SNOW PEA SPROUTS

Cook the rice noodles in boiling water for 1 minute then drain and set aside. Heat the oils in a wok over a high heat. Add the chilli pepper, spring onions and coriander and sauté for 1 minute. Add the oyster sauce, honey and ketchup manis and cook for 2 minutes.

Add the snow pea sprouts and rice noodles to the wok and sauté for 3 minutes or until heated through. Sprinkle with peanuts and serve with char-grilled chicken and a squeeze of lime.

SERVES 4

INGREDIENTS

435 g (14 oz) fresh rice noodles

1 teaspoon sesame oil

1 teaspoon peanut oil

1 fresh red chilli pepper, seeded and chopped

4 spring onions (scallions), chopped

1 teaspoon ground coriander

2 tablespoons oyster sauce

2 tablespoons honey

2 tablespoons ketchup manis

155 g (5 oz) snow pea (mangetout) sprouts

½ cup (75 g/2½ oz) chopped roasted unsalted peanuts

CUCUMBER AND CORIANDER SALAD

Slice the cucumbers into long strips using a vegetable peeler. Arrange the cucumber strips and coriander leaves on a serving plate and sprinkle with the sesame seeds.

Trim the beef of any fat or sinew. Heat the oil in a frying pan or skillet over a high heat. Add the beef and cook for 5–6 minutes or until cooked to your liking. Stand the beef for 5 minutes before slicing. Place the beef slices on top of the cucumber salad.

To make dressing, place all the ingredients in a bowl and mix well. Pour the dressing over the salad and serve warm.

SERVES 4 AS A FIRST COURSE

INGREDIENTS

3 Lebanese cucumbers

2 tablespoons coriander (cilantro) leaves

2 tablespoons toasted sesame seeds

500 g (1 lb) eye fillet of beef

2 teaspoons oil

Dressing

2 tablespoons soy sauce

2 tablespoons Thai sweet chilli sauce

2 teaspoons fish sauce

2 teaspoons sesame oil

Potatoes.

CHAPTER 6

Potatoes

GNOCCHI WITH GRILLED BLUE CHEESE SABAYON

INGREDIENTS

Gnocchi

500 g (1 lb) starchy potatoes, peeled and chopped

2 egg yolks

1 cup (125 g/4 oz) plain (all-purpose) flour

2 tablespoons chopped fresh sage leaves

cracked black pepper

Blue Cheese Sabayon

4 egg yolks

½ cup (125 mL/4 fl oz) chicken stock

185 g (6 oz) soft blue cheese

2 tablespoons light (single) cream

90 g (3 oz) butter, chopped

Place the potatoes in a saucepan of boiling water and simmer for 10 minutes or until tender. Drain the potatoes and place in a bowl. Mash them with a fork until smooth.

Add the egg yolks, flour, sage leaves and pepper to the mashed potatoes and mix to form a stiff dough. You may need to add extra flour to stiffen the dough. With floured hands, shape tablespoons of the dough into oval shapes and press the top with a fork to flatten slightly.

To cook gnocchi, place a few gnocchi at a time in a saucepan of boiling water and cook for 4 minutes or until the gnocchi have risen to the surface, drain well and place in a greased baking pan.

To make blue cheese sabayon, place the egg yolks and stock in a heatproof bowl over a saucepan of simmering water. Beat the egg yolks for 5 minutes or until they are very thick. Place the blue cheese and cream in another bowl and beat until smooth. Slowly add the blue cheese mixture to the egg yolks, beating well. Still holding the bowl over the simmering water, continue beating while gradually adding the butter, beating well to combine.

Pour the sabayon over the gnocchi in the baking pan and place under a hot preheated griller (broiler) for 2 minutes or until the sabayon is golden brown. Serve immediately with a rocket (arugula), Parmesan cheese and balsamic salad.

SERVES 4–6

SALT AND ROSEMARY BAKED POTATOES

INGREDIENTS

1 kg (2 lbs) starchy potatoes

2 tablespoons olive oil

sea salt

4 rosemary sprigs

Scrub the potatoes with a brush in plenty of water until they are clean and dry well. Cut the potatoes into wedges and place in a baking pan. Spoon over the olive oil, sprinkle well with salt and add the rosemary.

Bake in a preheated at oven 220°C (425°F) for 35–45 minutes or until the potatoes are crisp and golden.

SERVES 4–6

POTATO, OLIVE AND PARMESAN CHEESE SOUFFLE

This dish reminds me of relaxing Sunday evening dinners, wearing comfortable clothes and with my feet up on the lounge.

Grease an eight cup (2 litre/3¼ imp. pints) soufflé dish and sprinkle the sides and base with the Parmesan cheese. Chop the potatoes into small pieces and place in a saucepan of boiling water. Simmer the potatoes for 8 minutes or until tender. Drain and place in a bowl. Add the milk and mash the potatoes with a fork until smooth.

Melt the butter in a frying pan or skillet over a medium heat. Add the onions and garlic and cook for 4 minutes or until they are golden brown. Remove from the heat and add to the potatoes. Add the thyme and tarragon leaves, sour cream, extra milk, olives, Parmesan cheese and egg yolks. Mix the ingredients well to combine.

Place the egg whites in a bowl and beat until stiff peaks form. Fold a few spoonfuls of egg white through the potato mixture to lighten it, then fold through the remaining egg whites. Pour the mixture into the prepared soufflé dish and bake in a preheated oven at 200°C (390°F) for 45–55 minutes or until puffed and golden.

SERVES 6

INGREDIENTS

⅓ cup (45 g 1½ oz) grated Parmesan cheese

500 g (1 lb) creamy mashing potatoes, peeled

½ cup (125 mL/4 fl oz) milk

2 tablespoons butter

3 brown onions, chopped

2 garlic cloves, crushed

1 tablespoon chopped fresh thyme leaves

1 tablespoon chopped fresh tarragon leaves

1 cup (250 g/8 oz) sour cream

½ cup (125 mL/4 fl oz) milk, extra

½ cup (75 g/2½ oz) pitted marinated olives, chopped

⅓ cup (45 g/1½ oz) grated Parmesan cheese, extra

6 eggs, separated

BRAISED SAFFRON POTATOES

Great, cold night, stomach pleasing potatoes.

Place the water, vegetable stock, onions, saffron threads and cumin seeds in a saucepan over a high heat and bring to the boil. Add the potatoes and simmer for 8 minutes or until the potatoes are soft.

Remove the potatoes using a slotted spoon and allow the liquid to simmer until reduced by half. Return the potatoes and add the peas to the pan. Cook for 4 minutes or until the potatoes are heated through.

To serve, place the potatoes and saffron juices in a deep plate and top with Parmesan cheese shavings and a sprinkling of pepper. Finish with a crusty bread roll and slices of roast meats.

SERVES 4

INGREDIENTS

1 cup (250 mL/8 fl oz) water

2 cups (500 mL/16 fl oz) vegetable stock

4 baby (pearl) onions, halved

4 saffron threads

½ teaspoon cumin seeds

12 baby potatoes, halved

½ cup (60 g/2 oz) shelled baby peas

Parmesan cheese shavings

cracked black pepper

BEER BATTERED FISH WITH POTATO CRISPS

Crisp, lightly battered fish with crunchy potatoes. A refreshing squeeze of lemon and a subtle dollop of basil cream—perfect.

To make beer batter, place the flour in a bowl, add the beer and whisk until smooth. Place the egg whites in a bowl and beat until soft peaks form. Fold the egg whites into the beer mixture.

Heat the oil in a deep saucepan until smoking. The oil should be deep enough to contain the four fillets of fish with space between them. Plunge the fish fillets into the batter and fry them in the hot oil until they are golden and crisp and the fish is tender (approximately 4 minutes). Drain the fish on absorbent kitchen paper and keep warm.

Make the potato crisps by slicing the potatoes as thinly as possible. Fry in the hot oil until they are golden and crisp (approximately 4–5 minutes), then drain them on absorbent kitchen paper.

To make basil cream, place the basil leaves, vinegar, sour cream and pepper in a bowl and mix to combine.

To serve, sprinkle the fish and the potato crisps with sea salt and serve with lemon or lime wedges and basil cream.

SERVES 4

INGREDIENTS

Beer Batter
2 cups (250 g/8 oz) plain (all-purpose) flour
1⅓ cups (340 mL/11 fl oz) cold beer
2 egg whites

4 × 225 g (7 oz) firm white fish fillets
oil for deep frying
6 medium potatoes, peeled

Basil Cream
3 tablespoons chopped fresh basil leaves
1 tablespoon balsamic vinegar
½ cup (125 g/4 oz) sour cream
ground black pepper

sea salt
8 lemon or lime wedges

GARLIC POTATO PUREE

Another simple favourite using the ever so humble potato.

Peel the potatoes and chop them into small pieces. Place in a saucepan of boiling water and allow to boil for 6–8 minutes or until soft, drain well. Place the potatoes and sour cream in a bowl and mash with a fork until smooth.

Melt the butter in a saucepan over a low heat, add the garlic and cook until the garlic and butter are golden. Place spoonfuls of potato purée on serving plates then sprinkle with the pepper and chopped garlic chives. To serve, spoon over the garlic butter and serve immediately with roast meats or homemade sausages (page 109).

SERVES 6

INGREDIENTS

1 kg (2 lbs) waxy or creamy potatoes
½ cup (125 g/4 oz) light sour cream
3 tablespoons butter
2 garlic cloves, crushed
cracked black pepper
garlic chives

Beer battered fish with potato crisps.

PROSCIUTTO, POTATO AND GOAT'S CHEESE PIES

INGREDIENTS

6 creamy potatoes, peeled
2 garlic cloves, thinly sliced
60 g (2 oz) butter, melted
2 tablespoons chopped fresh sage leaves
6 slices prosciutto (Parma) ham, chopped
2 eggs, lightly beaten
1 cup (250 g/8 oz) sour cream
1 teaspoon cracked pink peppercorns
250 g (8 oz) soft goat's cheese, sliced

Crisp and creamy little pies to serve with anything! Great for picnics, cold.

Thinly slice the potatoes and place them in a bowl with the garlic, butter and sage leaves. Toss to combine. Grease and line the base of six 1 cup (250 mL/8 fl oz) capacity ramekins. Place layers of potatoes in each ramekin until all the potatoes have been used. Top the potatoes with the prosciutto. Place the eggs, sour cream and peppercorns in a bowl and whisk to combine. Pour evenly over the potatoes and top with slices of goat's cheese.

Bake in a preheated oven at 180°C (355°F) for 35–45 minutes or until the potatoes are soft and the tops are a deep golden brown. To serve, run a knife around the edge of the ramekins and place the pies on serving plates. Serve pies with char-grilled beef steaks.

SERVES 6

ONION AND POTATO FLAT BREADS

INGREDIENTS

1 quantity pizza dough (see page 170)

Topping
1 tablespoon olive oil
2 onions, sliced
2 tablespoons chopped fresh basil leaves
1 tablespoon seeded mustard
1 tablespoon olive oil, extra
3 waxy potatoes, peeled
cracked black pepper
½ cup (60 g/2 oz) grated Parmesan cheese

Divide the dough into six equal pieces and roll it out on a lightly floured surface until you have 4 mm (⅛ in) thick rounds. Place on greased baking sheets, cover and set aside.

Heat the oil in a frying pan or skillet over a high heat. Add the onions and sauté for 3 minutes or they until are soft. Remove the onions from the pan and stir through the basil leaves and mustard. Heat the extra oil in another frying pan over a medium heat. Slice the potatoes thinly and add to the pan. Cook the potatoes for 1 minute each side or until they are soft, remove from the heat.

Arrange the onion mixture and potatoes on the dough rounds, sprinkle with pepper and Parmesan cheese. Bake in a preheated oven at 220°C (425°F) for 25 minutes or until the breads are puffed and golden. Serve warm with tapénade or basil mayonnaise (page 113).

MAKES 6 BREADS

PESTO AND POTATO FRITTATA

Heat the oil in a frying pan or skillet over a medium heat. Add the potatoes and cook, stirring, for 8 minutes or until they are golden and soft. Add the spring onions, pine nuts, asparagus and sun-dried tomatoes and cook for 2 minutes.

Place the eggs, milk and pesto in a bowl and whisk to combine. Pour over the potato mixture in the pan and reduce the temperature to low. Sprinkle the frittata with the Parmesan cheese and cook for 6 minutes or until almost set.

Cook the frittata under a hot preheated griller (broiler) for 2 minutes or until the top is golden. To serve, cut the frittata into wedges and serve on slices of hot buttered sourdough bread.

SERVES 4

INGREDIENTS

1 tablespoon olive oil

375 g (12 oz) waxy potatoes, peeled and chopped

4 spring onions (scallions), chopped

¼ cup (30 g/1 oz) pine nuts

1 bunch asparagus, chopped

6 sun-dried tomatoes, sliced

6 eggs, lightly beaten

1 cup (250 mL/8 fl oz) milk

½ cup pesto (see page 169)

2 tablespoons grated Parmesan cheese

SPICED LAMB RACKS WITH CARAMELISED POTATOES

Trim the lamb and bone of any excess fat. Place the harissa, mint leaves, honey, mustard and lemon juice in a bowl and mix well to combine. Brush this mixture over the lamb racks, place in a covered dish and refrigerate to marinate for 4 hours. Place the lamb in a greased baking pan and bake in a preheated oven at 200°C (390°F) for 25–30 minutes or until the lamb is cooked to your liking.

To make caramelised potatoes, cut the unpeeled potatoes into small chunks and place in a saucepan of boiling water. Allow the potatoes to simmer for 8 minutes or until almost cooked. Drain the potatoes and dry them well.

Heat the oil in a frying pan or skillet over a medium heat. Add the onions, bay leaves and potatoes and cook, stirring, for 5 minutes or until the potatoes are golden. Add the sugar and salt and cook for a further minute then remove the bay leaves.

To serve, place the lamb racks on serving plates and serve with potatoes and steamed sugar snap peas or asparagus.

SERVES 4

INGREDIENTS

4 lamb racks (French ribbed chops) with 3 cutlets in each

1 teaspoon harissa (page 53)

2 tablespoons chopped fresh mint leaves

2 tablespoons honey

2 tablespoons seeded mustard

1 tablespoon lemon juice

Caramelised Potatoes

6 waxy potatoes, scrubbed

2 tablespoons olive oil

2 onions, chopped

2 bay leaves

1 teaspoon white granulated sugar

½ teaspoon sea salt

Berry fruits.

CHAPTER 7

Berry fruits

SMOKED CHICKEN WITH BLUEBERRY SALSA

INGREDIENTS

6 smoked chicken breast fillets
155 g (5 oz) rocket (arugula) leaves
1 avocado, sliced
2 vine-ripened tomatoes
155 g (5 oz) marinated feta cheese
2 tablespoons raspberry vinegar
cracked black pepper

Blueberry Salsa
250 g (8 oz) blueberries
½ mango, chopped
½ red onion, chopped
1 tablespoon soft brown sugar
3 tablespoons raspberry vinegar, extra

To smoke your own chicken, follow the smoking instructions for the beef (page 104). Chicken breasts will take approximately 20 minutes to smoke.

Arrange the chicken, rocket, avocado, tomatoes (cut into wedges) and feta cheese on individual serving plates. Sprinkle with vinegar and pepper.

To make blueberry salsa, place the blueberries, mango, onion, sugar and extra vinegar in a bowl and mix to combine.

To serve, place a mound of salsa on top or next to the chicken salad and serve with char-grilled olive bread.

SERVES 6

SEARED LAMB WITH GOOSEBERRIES

INGREDIENTS

750 g (1½ lbs) lamb fillets
1 tablespoon oil
cracked black pepper
2 tablespoons chopped fresh lemon thyme leaves

Gooseberry Sauce
2 teaspoons oil, extra
2 red onions, chopped
1 teaspoon grated fresh ginger
310 g (10 oz) gooseberries
1 cup (250 mL/8 fl oz) white wine
1 cup (250 mL/8 fl oz) chicken or veal stock
4 saffron threads

Trim the lamb fillets of any excess fat or sinew and then brush them with the oil and roll them in the pepper and lemon thyme leaves. Set aside.

Heat the extra oil in a saucepan over a medium heat. Add the onions and ginger and sauté for 3 minutes or until the onion is soft and golden. Add the gooseberries, wine, stock and saffron threads and bring to the boil. Reduce the heat and allow the mixture to simmer for 25 minutes or until the sauce has reduced by half.

To cook the lamb, heat a frying pan or skillet over a high heat. Add the lamb and cook for 2 minutes each side or until the outside is browned.

To serve, place the lamb on serving plates and top with the gooseberry sauce. Serve with crisp potatoes and steamed asparagus.

SERVES 4

CURRANT AND ROSE CREAM TARTS

Quaint little tarts to serve with flower teas.

Roll out the pastry on a lightly floured surface until 4 mm (⅙ in) thick. Cut the pastry to fit six 12 cm (5 in) removable base tart tins. Ease the pastry into the tins and trim off any excess. Line the tarts with nonstick baking parchment and fill with baking weights or rice. Place the tarts on a baking sheet. Bake in a preheated oven at 200°C (390°F) for 10 minutes. Remove the weights and parchment. Bake for a further 10 minutes or until golden brown. Set aside to cool completely.

To make rose cream, place the rose petals and water in a small saucepan over a low heat. Allow the roses to infuse their flavour into the water until there is only 1 tablespoon of liquid remaining. Strain the liquid and allow to cool.

Place the cream into a bowl and beat until thick. Fold through the rose liquid, icing sugar and raspberry purée. Fill the tarts with the rose cream and top with the red and white currants. Dust with icing sugar before serving.

MAKES 6 TARTS

INGREDIENTS

1 quantity sweet shortcrust pastry (page 168)

Rose Cream

12 fragrant rose petals

⅓ cup (90 mL/3 fl oz) water

1 cup (250 mL/8 fl oz) heavy (double) cream

1 tablespoon icing (confectioners') sugar

2 tablespoons raspberry purée

Topping

340 g (11 oz) mixed red and white currants

icing (confectioners') sugar for dusting

BALSAMIC SALAD

Place the berries, sugar and balsamic vinegar in a bowl and toss to combine. Refrigerate for 1 hour before serving.

To make vanilla biscuits, place the butter, vanilla extract and icing sugar in a bowl and beat until light and creamy. Sift the flours into the mixture and mix to a smooth dough.

Roll tablespoons of the mixture into balls and place on greased baking sheets. Flatten and bake in a preheated oven at 200°C (390°F) for 12–15 minutes or until golden. Let stand for 5 minutes before transferring to cool on wire racks.

To serve, divide the berries between four dessert plates and serve with heavy (double) cream and vanilla biscuits on the side.

SERVES 4

INGREDIENTS

600 g (1¼ lbs) mixed berries

⅓ cup (90 g/3 oz) white granulated sugar

⅓ cup (90 mL/3 fl oz) balsamic vinegar

Vanilla Biscuits

185 g (6 oz) butter

1 tablespoon vanilla extract

⅓ cup (60 g/2 oz) icing (confectioners') sugar

1 cup (125 g/4 oz) self-raising flour

1 cup (125 g/4 oz) plain (all-purpose) flour

Currant and rose cream tarts, Berry sponge with lavender cream and Hazelnut meringues with frosted berries.

BERRY SPONGE WITH LAVENDER CREAM

Place the sponge mixture into two greased 20 cm (8 in) round cake tins. Bake in a preheated oven at 180°C (355°F) for 20–25 minutes or until the cake comes away from the sides of the tins. Let stand for 2 minutes transferring to cool on wire racks.

To make filling, place the cream in a bowl and beat until whipped. Fold through the lavender flowers and icing sugar. Spread half the cream over one cake and top with half the berries. Top with the remaining cake, cream filling and berries.

To serve, decorate with chocolate curls and dust heavily with icing sugar. Serve sponge pieces with a selection of flower teas.

SERVES 6–8

INGREDIENTS

1 quantity sponge cake mixture (page 169)

Filling

1½ cups (375 mL/12 fl oz) heavy (double) cream

1 tablespoon lavender flowers

1 tablespoon icing (confectioners') sugar

2 teaspoons grated orange rind

225 g (7 oz) red raspberries

225 g (7 oz) golden raspberries

white chocolate curls

icing (confectioners') sugar for dusting

HAZELNUT MERINGUES WITH FROSTED BERRIES

To make meringues, place the caster sugar and water in a small saucepan and stir over a low heat until the sugar has dissolved. Increase the heat and simmer the syrup until it reaches hard ball stage.

While the syrup is simmering, beat the egg whites in a large bowl until soft peaks form. Add the syrup in a thin stream and continue beating. After the syrup has been added beat the meringue until cool.

Fold the hazelnuts through the meringue. Place six even piles of meringue on two greased baking sheets. With a knife, smooth the meringue into rounds with flat tops. Bake in a preheated oven at 120°C (245°F) for 50–60 minutes or until the meringues are dry and crisp. Turn the oven off and cool the meringues with the door ajar.

To make the filling, whisk together the mascarpone and crème de cassis. Spoon the mixture onto the tops of the cooled meringues.

To make topping, brush the berries with the egg white. Roll them in the caster sugar and place them on wire racks to dry.

To serve, arrange the frosted berries on top of the meringues and serve with raspberry purée swirled through heavy (double) cream.

SERVES 6

INGREDIENTS

Meringues

1⅓ cups (310 g/10 oz) caster (superfine) sugar

¾ cup (185 mL/6 fl oz) water

6 egg whites

½ cup (90 g/3 oz) hazelnuts, finely chopped

Filling

225 g (7 oz) mascarpone

2 tablespoons crème de cassis

Topping

225 g (7 oz) small strawberries

155 g (5 oz) cherries

155 g (5 oz) red currants

1 egg white, lightly beaten

caster (superfine) sugar

BLUEBERRY SOUR CREAM MUFFINS

INGREDIENTS

2 cups (250 g/8 oz) self-raising flour

⅓ cup (75 g/2½ oz) caster (superfine) sugar

2 eggs, lightly beaten

60 g (2 oz) butter, melted

1¼ cups (310 g/10 oz) sour cream

1 teaspoon vanilla extract

310g (10 oz) blueberries

2 teaspoons grated lemon rind

Lemon Butter

125 g (4 oz) butter

2 tablespoons lemon juice

3 tablespoons icing (confectioners') sugar

A lazy sunny morning, coffee and warm muffins with tangy lemon butter melting into them ...

Place the flour and caster sugar in a bowl and mix to combine. Place the eggs, butter, sour cream and vanilla extract in another bowl and beat until combined. Add in the flour mixture and stir until just combined, do not over mix. Fold through the blueberries and lemon rind.

Spoon the mixture into 1 cup (250 mL/8 fl oz) capacity greased muffin pans. Bake in a preheated oven at 200°C (390°F) for 25–30 minutes or until the muffins are cooked when tested with a skewer.

To make lemon butter, place the butter, lemon juice and icing sugar in a bowl and beat until light and fluffy.

Serve the muffins warm topped with the lemon butter.

MAKES 8 MUFFINS

FREE FORM BERRY GALETTES

INGREDIENTS

375 g (12 oz) ready-made puff pastry

Filling

½ cup (125 g/4 oz) cream cheese

2 tablespoons soft brown sugar

1 teaspoon vanilla extract

1 tablespoon orange juice

Topping

155 g (5 oz) raspberries

155 g (5 oz) strawberries

155 g (5 oz) blackberries

2 teaspoons grated orange rind

3 tablespoons white granulated sugar

These easy pastries are great for a brunch.

Cut the pastry into six equal pieces. Place each pastry on a lightly floured surface and roll into a random shape 4 mm (⅙ in) thick. Fold the edges of the pastry over to form an edge. Refrigerate until required.

To make filling, place the cream cheese, brown sugar, vanilla extract and orange juice in a bowl and mix well. Spread the filling over the pastry bases, leaving a 1 cm (⅓ in) border to the pastry edge.

To make topping, place the berries and orange rind in a bowl and toss gently to combine. Spoon over the filling and sprinkle well with sugar. Place the galettes on baking sheets and place in a preheated oven at 200°C (390°F) for 15 minutes or until the pastry is puffed and golden. Serve the galettes with rose cream (page 81).

MAKES 6

ANGEL FOOD CAKE WITH CHOCOLATE CREAM

To make cake, sift the flours and sugar together twice and set aside. Place the egg whites in a bowl and beat until soft peaks form. Continue beating and add the cream of tartar, beating until stiff peaks form. Add the extra sugar a little at a time and beat well. Beat in the vanilla extract. Fold the flour mixture through the egg whites and pour into a greased 25 cm (10 in) angel food cake tin. Bake in a preheated oven at 175°C (350°F) for 40–45 minutes or until the cake is cooked when tested with a skewer. Invert the cake while it is still in the tin and allow it to stand until cool.

Remove the cake from the tin. Fill the centre of the cake with raspberries and top with violets. Dust heavily with icing sugar.

To make chocolate cream, place the cream and the chocolate in a saucepan over a low heat and stir until it has melted. Allow the chocolate cream to cool and then beat until the mixture is light.

Serve cake with raspberries and a spoonful of chocolate cream.

SERVES 10

INGREDIENTS

¾ cup (90 g/3 oz) plain (all-purpose) flour

2 tablespoons cornflour (cornstarch)

½ cup (125 g/4 oz) white granulated sugar

12 egg whites

1 teaspoon cream of tartar

¾ cup (185 g/6 oz) white granulated sugar, extra

2 teaspoons vanilla extract

350 g (11 oz) raspberries

2 tablespoons violet flowers

3 tablespoons icing (confectioners') sugar

Chocolate Cream

½ cup (125 mL/4 fl oz) light (single) cream

125 g (4 oz) dark chocolate, chopped

CHOCOLATE AND RASPBERRY ICE CREAM

Place the egg yolks and caster sugar in a bowl and beat until light and fluffy. Gently fold in the whipped cream. In another bowl, beat the egg whites until stiff peaks form then fold them into the cream mixture. Fold the raspberries, chocolate and vanilla extract through the cream mixture and pour it into a metal container. Cover with plastic wrap (cling film) and freeze for 6 hours until firm.

To serve, place scoops of ice cream in dessert bowls, top with extra raspberries and serve with spiced hazelnut biscotti (page 161).

SERVES 6

INGREDIENTS

6 eggs, separated

1¼ cups (250 g/8 oz) caster (superfine) sugar

2½ cups (625 mL/20 fl oz) heavy (double) cream, whipped

310 g (10 oz) raspberries, crushed

155 g (5 oz) white chocolate, chopped

2 teaspoons vanilla extract

Garlic, onions and shallots.

CHAPTER 8

Garlic, onions and shallots

SMOKED MOZZARELLA BAKED ONIONS

INGREDIENTS

8 brown onions

Filling

250 g (8 oz) smoked mozzarella, grated
1 red capsicum (sweet pepper), roasted and chopped (page 170)
⅓ cup (60 g/2 oz) pitted olives, chopped
1 cup (60 g/2 oz) fresh breadcrumbs
olive oil
cracked black pepper

Peel the onions and scoop out the onion flesh, leaving a thick shell. Place the onions in a saucepan of boiling water and cook for 5 minutes or until they are softened slightly. Drain well and place on baking sheets.

To make filling, place the mozzarella, capsicum, olives and breadcrumbs in a bowl and mix to combine. Spoon the filling into the onions and press down firmly. Drizzle with olive oil and sprinkle with pepper. Bake in a preheated oven at 180°C (355°F) for 40 minutes or until soft and golden brown.

To serve, place the onions on a serving plate and serve with roasted meats or with bread and steamed greens for a vegetarian meal.

SERVES 4

CARAMELISED ONION TART

INGREDIENTS

1 quantity shortcrust pastry (page 168)

Filling

1 tablespoon butter
1 tablespoon olive oil
5 brown onions, sliced
3 tablespoons dry white wine
1 egg, lightly beaten
½ cup (125 g/4 oz) sour cream
1 tablespoon chopped fresh chervil leaves
cracked black pepper

Roll out the pastry to 4 mm (⅛ in) thick. Place the pastry in a 23 cm (9½ in) removable base tart tin, trim the edges and prick the base. Refrigerate for 10 minutes then line the pastry with nonstick baking parchment and fill with baking weights or rice. Bake in a preheated oven at 180°C (355°F) for 10 minutes. Remove the weights or rice and parchment and return to the oven for 5 minutes or until the pastry is lightly browned.

To make filling, melt the butter and heat the oil in a frying pan or skillet over a medium heat. Add the onions and cook, stirring, for 4 minutes or until soft. Reduce the temperature to low and cook, stirring occasionally, for 20 minutes or until the onions are caramelised. Stir in the wine and cook for 2 minutes. Set aside.

Place the egg, sour cream, chervil leaves and pepper in a bowl and whisk to combine. Pour into the pastry shell and top with the onions. Return to the oven and bake for 20 minutes or until the sour cream mixture is set.

To serve, cut the tart into wedges and serve warm with wedges of tomme fraîche and slices of pear or white peach.

SERVES 6

BEEF WITH RICH BERRY JUS

Break the garlic cloves from the heads and remove a few layers of the papery skin. Place 1 tablespoon of the oil in a baking pan and add the garlic, swirling the pan to coat the garlic. Tie the beef with string to hold its shape. Heat the remaining oil in a frying pan or skillet over a high heat, add the beef and cook for 1 minute each side or until it is browned and sealed on all sides.

Transfer the beef from the frying pan to the baking pan with the garlic. Combine the balsamic vinegar and port jelly in a small bowl. Brush this mixture over the beef to thickly coat it and sprinkle with pepper. Place the beef in a preheated oven and cook at 200°C (390°F) for 35–45 minutes or until the beef is cooked to your liking.

Remove the beef from the pan, place it on a carving board and cover it with aluminium foil. Remove the garlic from the pan, set it aside and keep warm. Place the berries in a food processor or blender and process until smooth. Stir the purée through a sieve to remove the seeds. Place the baking pan over a high heat on top of the stove. Stir well to loosen pan juices from the base of the pan. Add the berry purée, stock, port and rosemary leaves and allow the mixture to quickly simmer until the liquid has been reduced by half and thickened.

To serve, remove the string from the beef and slice. Place the beef and garlic on serving plates. Top with berry jus and serve with parsnip and brown butter purée (page 104).

SERVES 4–6

INGREDIENTS

2 heads garlic

2 tablespoons oil

750 g–850 g (1½ lbs) fillet of beef, trimmed of any sinew

3 tablespoons balsamic vinegar

3 tablespoons port jelly, warmed

cracked black pepper

310 g (10 oz) mixed berries

½ cup (125 mL/4 fl oz) beef stock

2 tablespoons port, extra

1 teaspoon fresh rosemary leaves

SWEET ONION MARMALADE

I keep a jar of this marmalade in the refrigerator. It adds a great finish to so many things—from sandwiches to curries and char-grilled meats.

Place all the ingredients in a saucepan over a low heat and stir until the sugar has dissolved. Increase the heat and simmer for 1½ hours or until the mixture is thick.

Allow the mixture to cool thoroughly and then pour it into hot sterilised jars and seal. Serve sweet onion marmalade on sandwiches, hamburgers, or as an accompaniment to a variety of dishes.

MAKES 6 CUPS

INGREDIENTS

8 brown onions, sliced

1 tablespoon cumin seeds

2 tablespoons yellow mustard seeds

4 fresh or dried curry leaves

2 cups (500 mL/16 fl oz) red wine vinegar

1 cup (155 g/5 oz) soft brown sugar

½ cup (90 g/3 oz) muscatels

GOLDEN SHALLOT CAKES WITH WARM GARLIC TAPENADE

INGREDIENTS

Shallot Cakes

1 tablespoon butter

4 golden shallots, peeled and chopped

¾ cup (90 g/3 oz) self-raising flour

1 egg

⅓ cup (90 mL/3 fl oz) milk

6 bocconcini, sliced

2 tablespoons fresh basil leaves

Garlic Tapénade

1 tablespoon olive oil

3 garlic cloves, crushed

1½ cups (225 g/7 oz) pitted green olives, chopped

2 teaspoons grated lemon rind

2 tablespoons balsamic vinegar

2 tablespoons chopped fresh parsley

I seeem to have lots of recipes 'to serve with drinks'. Just for the record, it's often easier and more fun to have friends over for drinks and lots of little things to eat than to do a whole dinner party meal.

To make shallot cakes, melt the butter in a frying pan or skillet over a medium heat. Add the shallots and cook for 2–3 minutes or until they are golden. Remove from the pan and set aside to cool.

Place the flour in a bowl. Whisk in the egg, milk and shallot mixture. Cook spoonfuls of the mixture in a greased frying pan over a medium heat for 1 minute each side or until golden. Keep warm.

To make garlic tapénade, heat the oil in a frying pan over a medium heat, add the garlic and cook for 2 minutes or until golden. Place the garlic, olives, lemon rind, balsamic vinegar and parsley in a food processor or blender and process until finely chopped. Place the mixture in a frying pan over a low heat and cook, stirring, for 1 minute or until it is heated through.

To serve, top each shallot cake with bocconcini and basil leaves. Spoon over some warm garlic tapénade and serve immediately.

SERVES 6

Golden shallot cakes with warm garlic tapenade and Golden garlic and onion risotto.

GOLDEN GARLIC AND ONION RISOTTO

INGREDIENTS

1 tablespoon olive oil

3 garlic cloves, crushed

3 brown onions, sliced

⅓ cup (90 mL/3 fl oz) white wine vinegar

2 tablespoons soft brown sugar

2 teaspoons fresh rosemary leaves

1 tablespoon olive oil, extra

2 cups (435 g/14 oz) Arborio rice

3 cups (750 mL/24 fl oz) vegetable stock

1 cup (250 mL/8 fl oz) dry white wine

125 g (4 oz) Gorgonzola, crumbled

cracked black pepper

Heat the oil in a frying pan or skillet over a medium heat. Add the garlic and onions and cook for 3 minutes or until they are soft and golden. Reduce the heat to low and add the vinegar, brown sugar and rosemary leaves. Allow the onions to cook slowly for 5 minutes or until they are very soft and caramelised, stirring occasionally. Set aside.

Heat the extra oil in a saucepan over a medium heat. Add the rice and cook, stirring, for 3 minutes or until the rice is translucent. Pour the stock and wine into another saucepan and bring to the boil. Keep the liquid hot while cooking the risotto. Add the stock mixture to the rice 1 cup at a time, stirring constantly. Continue adding stock 1 cup at a time until all the stock has been absorbed and the rice is tender and creamy. Stir in the onion mixture and cook for 1 minute to heat through.

To serve, place the risotto in deep bowls and top with Gorgonzola and a good sprinkling of pepper. Serve with warm bread and a glass of full bodied red wine.

SERVES 4

GARLIC SMOTHERED LAMB

INGREDIENTS

1½ kg (3 lbs) leg lamb, boned and tied

Garlic Paste

4 garlic cloves, crushed

¾ cup (90 g/3 oz) pine nuts

3 tablespoons lemon juice

1 teaspoon cumin seeds

Whenever I have a craving for a well-flavoured roast and vegetables, this is what I cook.

Trim the lamb of any excess fat or sinew and place it in a greased baking pan.

To make garlic paste, place all the ingredients in a food processor or blender and process until smooth. Spread the garlic paste over the lamb, cover and refrigerate for 4 hours to allow the flavours to develop. Bake the lamb in a preheated oven at 200°C (390°F) for 1¼ hours or until the lamb is cooked to your liking.

To serve, cover the lamb and allow it to stand for 5 minutes before cutting the string and carving. Serve with parsnip and brown butter purée (page 104) and steamed snake beans.

SERVES 4–6

ROAST GARLIC AND ONION SOUP

A great recipe for a cold Sunday afternoon, while sitting listening to the rain.

Place the onions in a baking pan and drizzle with the oil. Bake in a preheated oven at 170°C (340°F) for 1 hour. Add the garlic to the pan and bake for a further 30 minutes or until the onions and garlic are soft. Peel and chop the onions and squeeze the garlic from their skins.

Heat the extra oil in a saucepan over a medium heat. Add the onion and garlic and cook for 3 minutes. Add the stock, sweet potato, lemon thyme leaves and chilli pepper to the pan and simmer for 30 minutes.

Pour the mixture in batches into a food processor or blender and process until smooth. Return to the saucepan and stir until heated through.

To make pesto croûtons, place the bread under a hot preheated griller (broiler) and toast on one side until golden. Spread the remaining side with pesto and grill until golden and crisp.

To serve, ladle the soup into warmed bowls and serve pesto croûtons on the side.

SERVES 4–6

INGREDIENTS

4 onions, unpeeled

1 tablespoon olive oil

10 garlic cloves, unpeeled

2 teaspoons olive oil, extra

6 cups (1.5 litres/2½ imp. pints) vegetable stock

155 g (5 oz) white sweet potato, peeled and chopped

1 tablespoon chopped fresh lemon thyme leaves

1 fresh red chilli pepper, seeded and chopped

Pesto Croûtons

12 slices crusty Italian bread

¾ cup pesto (page 169)

BRAISED SPRING ONIONS

Trim and peel the onions leaving about 6 cm (2½ in) of stem intact. Cut the onions in half lengthwise. Heat the oil in a frying pan or skillet over a medium heat. Add the onions to the pan and cook for 4 minutes each side or until they are golden brown.

Add the remaining ingredients to the pan, reduce the heat to a simmer and allow the onions to slowly braise for 30 minutes or until they are soft and golden.

To serve, place the onions on serving plates and serve with slices of roast suckling pork and sautéed apples.

SERVES 6

INGREDIENTS

12 spring onions (scallions)

2 teaspoons oil

1 cup (250 mL/8 fl oz) red wine

1 cup (250 mL/8 fl oz) vegetable stock

1 clove

1 bay leaf

1 piece lemon rind

1 piece cassia bark (cinnamon)

1 teaspoon coriander seeds

Garlic lobster tails with grilled limes and aioli and Roast garlic papadelle.

GARLIC LOBSTER TAILS WITH GRILLED LIMES AND AIOLI

Grilled limes easily release their juice and it slightly caramelises on the grill.

Melt the butter in a saucepan over a low heat. Add the garlic, lime juice, coriander leaves and cumin and heat until golden. Brush over the lobster tails and place them on a hot preheated barbecue or char-griller, flesh side down, for 45 seconds then shell side down for 1–2 minutes or until cooked through. Cook the limes on the barbecue or char-griller flesh side down, for 1½ minutes or until golden.

To make aïoli, place all the ingredients in a bowl and mix to combine.

To serve, place the lobster tails on serving plates, sprinkle with pepper and serve with warm grilled limes, aïoli and a salad of rocket (arugula) and baby endive (frisée).

SERVES 4

INGREDIENTS

90 g (3 oz) butter
2 garlic cloves, crushed
2 tablespoons lime juice
2 teaspoons chopped fresh coriander (cilantro) leaves
½ teaspoon ground cumin
4 baby lobster tails, halved
cracked black pepper
4 limes, halved

Aïoli
1 quantity whole egg mayonnaise (page 169)
4 garlic cloves, crushed
2 tablespoons chopped fresh basil leaves

ROAST GARLIC PAPPARDELLE

Place the garlic on a baking sheet and toss with the oil. Bake in a preheated oven at 170°C (340°F) for 30 minutes or until the garlic is soft and golden. Squeeze and peel the garlic from their skins and set aside. Place the pappardelle in a saucepan of boiling water and simmer for 5–10 minutes or until tender. Drain and keep warm.

Place the prosciutto under a hot preheated griller (broiler) and grill for 1 minute each side or until crisp. Break into small pieces and set aside. Melt the butter in a frying pan or skillet over a medium heat. Add the breadcrumbs and cook, stirring, for 3 minutes or until they are golden and toasted. Add the garlic, prosciutto, thyme leaves, sage leaves, bocconcini and anchovies and toss to combine. Cook for 2 minutes or until heated through.

To serve, toss the garlic mixture with the hot pappardelle and serve in deep pasta bowls with red wine and crusty Italian bread.

SERVES 4

INGREDIENTS

20 unpeeled garlic cloves
2 teaspoons oil
500 g (1 lb) pappardelle
8 slices prosciutto (Parma) ham
2 tablespoons butter
2 cups (125 g/4 oz) fresh breadcrumbs
1 tablespoon fresh thyme leaves
1 tablespoon chopped fresh sage leaves
8 baby bocconcini
6 anchovies (optional)

HAMBURGERS WITH RED WINE ONIONS

INGREDIENTS

4 fillet steaks, 2.5 cm (1 in) thick

olive oil

cracked black pepper

4 slices aged cheddar cheese

8 thick slices crusty bread, toasted

Red Wine Onions

2 teaspoons oil

2 onions, peeled and cut into wedges

½ cup (125 mL/4 fl oz) red wine

2 tablespoons honey

1 tablespoon chopped fresh tarragon leaves

2 teaspoons yellow mustard seeds

What else can I say? Sometimes you just have to have a fillet steak hamburger with melting cheese and lots of red wine onions.

Brush the steaks with the oil and sprinkle with the pepper. Place on a hot preheated char-griller or barbecue and cook for 1–2 minutes each side or until cooked to your liking. Place the steaks on a baking sheet and top with cheddar cheese. Place under a hot preheated griller (broiler) for 1 minute or until the cheese is bubbling.

To make red wine onions, heat the oil in a frying pan or skillet over a medium heat. Add the onions and cook for 4 minutes or until golden. Add the rest of the ingredients and reduce the heat to a simmer. Simmer for 15 minutes or until the onions are very soft.

To serve, place the steaks on the toasted bread and top with loads of red wine onions and the remaining toast slices.

SERVES 4

SPRING ONION TORTILLA

INGREDIENTS

1 tablespoon butter

6 spring onions (scallions), sliced

6 slices spicy salami

2 potatoes, peeled and chopped

6 eggs, lightly beaten

1¼ cups (310 mL/10 fl oz) milk

1 tablespoon chopped fresh oregano leaves

½ cup (60 g/2 oz) grated Parmesan cheese

A great recipe for a weekend lunch or a picnic.

Melt the butter in a frying pan or skillet over a medium heat. Add the spring onions, salami and potatoes and cook, stirring occasionally, for 8 minutes or until the potatoes are tender. Place the eggs, milk, oregano and Parmesan cheese in a bowl and whisk well to combine.

Pour the egg mixture over the spring onion mixture, reduce the temperature to low and cook for 5 minutes or until almost set. Place the tortilla under a hot preheated griller (broiler) for 1 minute or until golden.

To serve, cut the tortilla into wedges and serve on toasted herbed bread with tomato jam.

SERVES 4

RED ONION PIZZAS

Individual, crunchy red onion pizzas topped with smoked salmon!

Divide the dough into four equal portions. Place on a lightly floured surface and roll out to 4 mm (⅛ in) thick. Place on lightly greased baking sheets and set aside until required.

To make topping, place the oil and onions in a baking pan and sprinkle with a little sea salt and the sage leaves. Cover the baking pan and bake in a preheated oven at 180°C (355°F) for 20 minutes or until the onions are soft.

Sprinkle the pizza bases with Gruyère cheese and top with the artichokes, onions and olives. Increase the oven temperature to 200°C (390°F) and bake the pizzas for 20 minutes or until the crusts are golden and crisp.

To serve pizzas, top with a spoonful of sour cream and a few slices of smoked salmon. Serve immediately.

SERVES 4

INGREDIENTS

1 quantity pizza dough (page 170)

Topping

2 teaspoons olive oil

3 red onions, peeled and cut into wedges

sea salt

2 tablespoons fresh sage leaves

1 cup (125 g/4 oz) grated Gruyère cheese

4 marinated artichoke hearts, quartered

⅔ cup (90 g/3 oz) marinated olives

GRILLED GARLIC POLENTA

Creamy polenta with a crunchy top of sage, Parmesan cheese and garlic. Perfect for an antipasto platter.

Pour the stock into a saucepan over a high heat and bring to the boil. Gradually add the polenta, stirring constantly, and cook for 20 minutes or until the polenta comes away from the sides of the saucepan. Stir in the butter and cream then spread the polenta into a greased 23 cm (9 in) square shallow cake tin.

Brush the top of the polenta with the butter and sprinkle with the sage leaves, Parmesan cheese, garlic and pepper. Place under a preheated medium griller (broiler) and cook the polenta for 6 minutes or until it is brown and heated through.

To serve, cut into small wedges and serve with an antipasto platter.

SERVES 6

INGREDIENTS

2 cups (500 mL/16 fl oz) vegetable stock

1 cup (185 g/6 oz) polenta (cornmeal)

60 g (2 oz) butter

½ cup (125 mL/4 fl oz) light (single) cream

Topping

30 g (1 oz) butter, melted

1 tablespoon fresh sage leaves

½ cup (60 g/2 oz) grated Parmesan cheese

3 garlic cloves, thinly sliced

cracked black pepper

Winter vegetables.

CHAPTER 9

Winter vegetables

CELERIAC AND BLUE BRIE SOUFFLES

INGREDIENTS

500 g (1 lb) celeriac, peeled and chopped
¼ cup (60 mL/2 fl oz) milk
2 tablespoons butter
125 g (4 oz) blue brie, chopped
cracked black pepper
1 tablespoon chopped fresh mint leaves
½ cup (125 g/4 oz) light sour cream
6 eggs, separated

The subtle flavour of celeriac gives this soufflé its wonderful taste.

Boil the celeriac until tender, drain, place in a bowl and mash with the milk and butter. Stir through the brie, pepper, mint, sour cream and egg yolks.

Place the egg whites in a bowl and beat until stiff peaks form. Fold the egg whites through the celeriac mixture.

Pour the mixture into six greased and collared 1 cup (250 mL/ 8 fl oz) capacity ramekins or soufflé dishes. Place the ramekins on a baking sheet and bake the soufflés in a preheated oven at 200°C (390°F) for 20 minutes or until they are puffed and golden on top. Serve immediately.

SERVES 6

WASABI SALMON WITH SESAME BOK CHOY

INGREDIENTS

2 teaspoons wasabi paste
2 tablespoons lime juice
2 teaspoons fish sauce
1 tablespoon soy sauce
2 tablespoons oil
4 salmon cutlets or steaks

Sesame Bok Choi
1 tablespoon sesame oil
2 tablespoons sesame seeds
1 garlic clove, crushed
340 g (11oz) baby bok choy, trimmed
3 tablespoons ketchup manis

A dish which combines clean and zesty Asian flavours.

Combine the wasabi, lime juice, fish sauce and soy sauce in a bowl and brush well over the salmon. Heat the oil in a large frying pan or skillet over a medium heat. Add the salmon and cook for 2 minutes each side or until cooked. Brush the salmon with the remaining marinade while cooking.

To make sesame bok choy, place the sesame oil in a frying pan, skillet or wok over a medium heat. Add the sesame seeds and garlic and sauté until golden. Add the bok choy and ketchup manis and sauté for 3 minutes or until tender. Arrange the salmon and bok choy on individual serving plates and serve immediately.

SERVES 4

SUGAR BAKED ARTICHOKES WITH AVOCADO SALSA

Different! The artichokes are great as a first course or as a light meal served with a leaf salad.

Scrub the artichokes well in cold water and place them in a baking pan. Sprinkle over the oil and salt and shake the pan to coat the artichokes. Bake the artichokes in a preheated oven at 200°C (390°F) for 30 minutes. Sprinkle them with the sugar and bake them for a further 15–20 minutes or until the artichokes are tender and golden.

Place the artichokes on individual serving plates. Divide the avocado between the plates. To make avocado salsa, combine the yoghurt, lemon or lime juice, chilli pepper and coriander leaves and pour the mixture over the avocado. Serve immediately.

SERVES 4

INGREDIENTS

475 g (15 oz) Jerusalem artichokes

2 tablespoons extra virgin olive oil

1 teaspoon sea salt

3 teaspoons white granulated sugar

Avocado Salsa

1 avocado, peeled and sliced

¼ cup (45 g/1½ oz) plain yoghurt

2 teaspoons lemon or lime juice

1 fresh red chilli pepper, seeded and chopped

1 tablespoon chopped fresh coriander (cilantro) leaves

SNAKE BEANS WITH COUS COUS

Theis dish can be served as a meal in itself or as an accompaniment to a spiced meat dish.

Place the cous cous in a bowl and pour over the boiling water. Allow the cous cous to stand for 5 minutes or until the water has been absorbed.

Heat the oil in a frying pan or skillet over a high heat. Add the onion, garlic and mustard seeds and sauté for 4 minutes or until the onion is golden. Add the snake beans and sauté for a further 5 minutes or until the beans have softened slightly. Toss through the hazelnuts.

Heat the extra oil in a frying pan over a high heat. Add the tomatoes and cook for 3 minutes. Toss through the basil leaves, capers and cous cous and cook for 3 minutes or until heated through.

To serve, place a bed of the cous cous mixture onto individual serving plates and top with the bean mixture. Serve with a spoonful of harissa (page 53) or chilli jam (page 47).

SERVES 4

INGREDIENTS

1 cup (200 g/6½ oz) cous cous

1/¼ cups (310 mL/10 fl oz) boiling water

1 tablespoon olive oil

1 onion, cut into wedges

2 garlic cloves, crushed

1 tablespoon black mustard seeds

500 g (1 lb) snake beans, trimmed and halved

225 g (7oz) hazelnuts, roasted and roughly chopped

1 tablespoon extra olive oil,

2 tomatoes, chopped

2 tablespoons chopped fresh basil leaves

2 tablespoons baby capers, rinsed

WINTER VEGETABLE CHIPS

INGREDIENTS

250 g (8 oz) parsnips, peeled
250 g (8 oz) celeriac, peeled
250 g (8 oz) swede, peeled
250 g (8 oz) sweet potato (kumera), peeled
250 g (8 oz) beetroot, peeled
vegetable oil for deep frying
sea salt

Remember, it is not a sin occasionally to deep fry!

Slice the parsnip, celeriac, swede, sweet potato and beetroot thinly with a wide vegetable peeler or a sharp knife. Half fill a medium saucepan with oil and bring it to the boil over a medium heat. Place the vegetable slices, a few at a time, in the hot oil and deep fry until golden and crisp. The cooking time will vary according to the vegetable. Drain on absorbent kitchen paper and keep the chips warm in an oven preheated to 150°C (300°F).

To serve, sprinkle the chips with sea salt and serve with tomato jam, chilli sauce or whole egg mayonnaise (page 169).

SERVES 4

ZUCCHINI PIZZETTAS

INGREDIENTS

1 quantity pizza dough (page 170)

Topping
2 teaspoons olive oil
2 garlic cloves, crushed
2 green zucchini (courgettes), sliced
2 yellow zucchini (courgettes), sliced
125 g (4 oz) sun-dried capsicums (sweet peppers), finely chopped
125 g (4 oz) ricotta cheese
2 fresh red chilli peppers, chopped
1 tablespoon toasted cumin seeds, lightly crushed
6 slices prosciutto (Parma) ham, torn into small pieces
½ cup (75 g/2½ oz) Niçoise olives
2 tablespoons fresh oregano leaves
cracked black pepper

Divide the pizza dough into four pieces and roll each piece on a lightly floured surface until the pastry is 7mm (¼ in) thick. Set aside.

Heat the oil in a frying pan or skillet over a high heat. Add the garlic and green and yellow zucchini and sauté for 3 minutes or until the vegetables are soft. Set aside to cool slightly.

Place the capsicums, ricotta cheese, chilli peppers and cumin seeds in a bowl and mix well to combine. Spread this mixture over the dough bases leaving a 1cm (⅓ in) border around the edge.

Top the pizzas with the zucchini mixture and sprinkle with the prosciutto, olives, oregano leaves and pepper. To cook the pizzas, preheat a pizza tile or baking sheets in a 200°C (390°F) oven. Slide the pizzas onto the tile or baking sheets. Cook for 20–30 minutes or until the bases are crisp and golden. Serve with a mixed green salad.

SERVES 4

Winter vegetable chips.

SMOKED BEEF WITH BAKED FENNEL

INGREDIENTS

300 g (9½ oz) smoking (hicory) chips
1½ kg (3 lbs) whole fillet beef
olive oil
1 garlic clove, halved
2 tablespoons olive oil, extra
1 tablespoon yellow mustard seeds
1 teaspoon coriander seeds
2 fennel bulbs, trimmed
8 garlic cloves
1 cup (250 mL/8 fl oz) dry white wine
cracked black pepper

This recipe will change your barbecue into a seriously respected piece of cooking equipment.

Soak the smoking chips in water for at least 30 minutes. Trim the beef of any excess fat and brush it with the oil. Rub the beef with the garlic clove halves and place the meat in a baking pan. Place the pan in a kettle or covered barbecue over white hot coals and allow it to cook, covered, for 20 minutes.

Place the extra oil, mustard seeds, coriander seeds, fennel, garlic and wine in a baking pan and place next to the beef in the barbecue. Drain the smoking chips and place them on the coals. Cover the barbecue and cook for a further 35 minutes or until the beef is cooked to your liking.

Serve the beef sliced on a bed of the baked fennel slices and sprinkle well with freshly cracked black pepper.

SERVES 6–8

PARSNIP AND BROWN BUTTER PUREE

INGREDIENTS

500 g (1 lb) parsnips, peeled and chopped
½ cup (125 mL/4 fl oz) light (single) cream
⅓ cup (90 mL/3 fl oz) chicken stock
60 g (2 oz) butter
2 garlic cloves, crushed
cracked black pepper

A simple recipe but one that tastes so good.

Boil the parsnips until they are tender, drain and then place them in a food processor or blender with the cream and stock and process until smooth. Keep the mixture warm.

Place the butter in a saucepan over a low heat and let it simmer for 5 minutes or until it is golden. Add the garlic to the pan.

Spoon the parsnip purée onto individual serving plates, drizzle with the browned butter and top with pepper. Serve with char-grilled or roasted meats.

SERVES 4

CHAR-GRILLED BEEF WITH SWEDE PUDDINGS

A recipe for those times which call for warming comfort food.

To make swede puddings, grease four 1 cup (250 mL/8 fl oz) capacity ramekins or moulds. Place the swede, garlic and shallots in layers in the ramekins. Pour the butter over mixture in the ramekins and sprinkle with Parmesan cheese. Bake in a preheated oven at 180°C (355°F) for 30–35 minutes or until the puddings are soft and golden.

Rub the steaks with the pepper and place them on a hot char-grill or in a hot char-grill pan. Cook for 2 minutes on each side or until cooked to your liking.

To serve, unmould the puddings and serve with the char-grilled steaks.

SERVES 4

INGREDIENTS

4 fillet steaks
cracked black pepper

Swede Puddings
500 g (1 lb) swede, peeled and thinly sliced
2 garlic cloves, sliced
4 golden shallots, peeled and sliced
90 g (3 oz) butter melted
⅓ cup (45 g/1½ oz) grated Parmesan cheese

CRISP SWEET POTATO GRIDDLE CAKES

Griddle cakes are a great Sunday night food.

Grate the sweet potato into a bowl. Add the chives, eggs, flour, coriander, Parmesan cheese and sour cream and mix well. Oil a hot griddle or a frying pan or skillet and place spoonfuls of the mixture onto the griddle and flatten them with a spatula. Cook for 3 minutes each side or until golden and crisp. Keep the griddle cakes warm. Repeat the cooking process with the remaining mixture.

To make yoghurt sauce, place the yoghurt, chilli sauce, coriander, cumin and orange rind in a bowl and mix to combine.

To serve, place the sweet potato griddle cakes in stacks on individual serving plates and serve accompanied by small individual bowls of yoghurt sauce.

SERVES 4–6

INGREDIENTS

750 g (1½ lbs) orange sweet potato (kumera), peeled
3 tablespoons chopped fresh chives
2 eggs, lightly beaten
2 tablespoons plain (all-purpose) flour
2 teaspoons ground coriander
½ cup (60 g/2 oz) grated Parmesan cheese
2 tablespoons sour cream
oil for cooking

Yoghurt Sauce
¾ cup (155 g/5 oz) thick plain yoghurt
3 tablespoons sweet chilli sauce
1 tablespoon chopped fresh coriander (cilantro) leaves
1 teaspoon ground cumin

PUMPKIN AND FETA RAVIOLI

INGREDIENTS

1 quantity poppyseed pasta (page 169)

1 egg, lightly beaten

Filling

340 g (11 oz) pumpkin, peeled and chopped

2 tablespoons butter

½ teaspoon grated nutmeg

½ teaspoon ground cumin

2 tablespoons plain (all-purpose) flour

225 g (7 oz) feta cheese, crumbled

Butter Sauce

90 g (3 oz) butter, extra

1 tablespoon fresh coriander (cilantro) leaves

cracked black pepper

pecorino cheese

Pasta with a crunch filled with spiced pumpkin and feta cheese is well worth the effort of preparation.

Roll out the pasta in a pasta machine or use a rolling pin to roll it out to 1–2 mm thickness and set aside, covering it with plastic wrap (cling film) or a tea towel so that the pasta does not dry out.

To make filling, boil the pumpkin until tender, drain and then mash it with the butter, nutmeg and cumin. Stir through the flour and feta. cheese. Mark the pasta with a knife to form 8 cm (3 in) squares and then place a spoonful of the mixture on half of the squares. Brush around the filling with the egg and then place the remaining pasta squares over the top of the filling. Crimp the edges with a fork or a pasta wheel.

To cook the pasta, place it in a saucepan of boiling water and cook for 4 minutes or until the pasta is tender, drain and keep warm. To make butter sauce, place the butter and the coriander leaves in a saucepan and cook over a low heat for 3 minutes or until the butter is lightly browned. To serve, place the pasta on a serving plate and pour over the sauce. Top with pepper and shaved pecorino cheese.

SERVES 4–6

JAPANESE BEETROOT STIR-FRY

INGREDIENTS

1 tablespoon hazelnut oil

1 tablespoon finely sliced fresh pink ginger

2 small leeks, sliced

4 beetroot, peeled

3 tablespoons shoyu

1 teaspoon wasabi paste

3 tablespoons sake

1 tablespoon white granulated sugar

6 nori sheets (dried seaweed)

Heat the hazelnut oil in a frying pan or skillet over a medium heat. Add the ginger and leeks and sauté for 4 minutes or until the leeks are soft and golden. Slice the beetroot and then cut the slices in half. Add the beetroot to the pan with the shoyu, wasabi, sake and sugar and stir-fry for 5–7 minutes or until the beetroot is slightly soft. Toast both sides of the nori sheets under a preheated griller (broiler) until crisp (approximately 30 seconds each side).

To serve, place the nori on individual serving plates and top with the beetroot stir-fry. Serve accompanied by slices of raw tuna and pickled Japanese vegetables.

SERVES 6

Pumpkin and feta ravioli.

WARM SALAD OF SPINACH AND PECORINO

INGREDIENTS

475 g (15 oz) English spinach leaves

1 pear, cored and sliced

225 g (7 oz) cherry tomatoes, halved

225 g (7 oz) pecorino cheese, shaved into pieces

155 g (5 oz) croûtons

Warm Dressing

3 tablespoons olive oil

2 red onions, sliced

3 tablespoons red wine vinegar

2 tablespoons water

1 tablespoon chopped fresh tarragon leaves

freshly ground black pepper

Easy, simple and a 'they'll be here any minute' type recipe.

Arrange the spinach, pear, tomatoes, pecorino cheese and croûtons on a serving plate.

To make dressing, heat the oil in a frying pan or skillet over a medium heat. Add the onions and cook for 3 minutes. Reduce the heat to low and add the vinegar and water. Allow the onions to simmer for a further 4 minutes or until they are soft.

Stir through the tarragon leaves and pour the dressing over the salad. Sprinkle over the pepper and serve immediately.

SERVES 4

CARAMELISED LEEK AND AGED CHEDDAR TARTS

INGREDIENTS

1 quantity shortcrust pastry (page 168)

Filling

2 tablespoons butter

4 leeks, sliced

½ teaspoon ground cumin

2 tablespoons brandy

2 eggs, lightly beaten

¾ cup (155 g/5 oz) sour cream

¾ cup (155g/5 oz) grated aged cheddar cheese

cracked black pepper

A glass of red wine and an open fire are the perfect accompaniments to this dish.

Roll the pastry out onto a lightly floured surface until the pastry is 2 mm (⅛ in) thick. Place the pastry into six 12 cm (5 in) removable base tart tins and line with baking parchment. Fill the pastry shells with baking weights or rice and bake at 180°C (355°F) for 10 minutes. Remove the weights or rice and parchment and bake for a further 5 minutes or until lightly golden.

To make filling, melt the butter in a frying pan over a low heat. Add the leeks, cumin and brandy and cook for 8 minutes or until the leeks are golden and caramelised. Set aside to cool. Place the eggs, sour cream, cheddar cheese and leek mixture in a bowl and mix to combine. Spoon the filling into pastry cases, sprinkle with pepper and bake at 180°C (355°F) for 15 minutes or until the filling is firm. Serve warm or cold with a rocket (arugula) salad.

SERVES 6

BEEF AND PORCINI SAUSAGES WITH MASH

Making sausages takes some time but the results make the effort worthwhile. It's also lots of fun.

Place the porcini mushrooms in a bowl and pour over the boiling water. Allow to stand for 40 minutes or until the mushrooms are soft. Drain the mushrooms into a strainer, reserve the liquid and press any excess liquid from the mushrooms.

Chop the mushrooms and place them in a bowl with the minced beef, breadcrumbs, egg, rosemary leaves and pepper and mix well to combine. Pull the sausage casing over the opening of a funnel or use a sausage maker. Press the mixture through the funnel to allow the casing to slide off the funnel with the filling inside.

Continue stuffing the casings until all the mixture has been used and then tie off both ends. Make twists in the sausage every 10 cm (4 in) to form small sausages. Place the sausages in a covered dish and refrigerate for 1 hour so that the sausages can set.

Blanch the sausages in simmering water for 5 minutes, drain and cut into small groups or into individual sausages. Cook the sausages over a medium heat in a lightly greased frying pan or skillet turning regularly, for 4 minutes or until the sausages are well browned and cooked through.

To make mash, pour the reserved mushroom water into a saucepan leaving any sediment behind. Top up with water until the saucepan is one-third full, place over a medium heat and allow to slow boil. Chop the potatoes into small chunks and add them to the saucepan. Cook for 6 minutes or until soft, drain and place in a bowl.

Add the butter and mash the potatoes with a fork until smooth. Stir in the cream and sorrel leaves.

To serve, place sausages on serving plates and serve hot with a pile of mash and some homemade tomato sauce or chutney.

SERVES 4

INGREDIENTS

60 g (2 oz) dried porcini (cèpes) mushrooms

2 cups (500 mL/16 fl oz) boiling water

650 g (1¼ lbs) quality minced (ground) beef

1 cup (60 g/2 oz) fresh breadcrumbs

1 egg, lightly beaten

2 teaspoons, chopped fresh rosemary leaves

cracked black pepper

sausage casings (ask your butcher)

Mash

5 creamy mashing potatoes, peeled

2 tablespoons butter

2 tablespoons light (single) cream

1 tablespoon chopped fresh sorrel leaves

Eggplant

CHAPTER 10

Eggplants

SMOKED CHEDDAR FRITTATA WITH EGGPLANT PUREE

INGREDIENTS

2 teaspoons olive oil

2 leeks, sliced

2 chorizo or spicy sausages, sliced

2 egg-shaped (Roma/plum) tomatoes, chopped

6 eggs

1 cup (250 mL/8 fl oz) milk

½ cup (125 g/4 oz) light sour cream

cracked black pepper

2 tablespoons chopped fresh parsley

250 g (8 oz) smoked cheddar cheese, roughly chopped

Eggplant Purée

2 small eggplants (aubergines)

sea salt

3 tablespoons lemon juice

1 garlic clove, crushed

1 teaspoon ground cumin

30 g (1 oz) butter, chopped

½ cup (125 mL/4 fl oz) light (single) cream

To make frittata, heat the oil in a frying pan or skillet over a medium heat. Add the leeks and cook for 6 minutes or until they are soft and golden. Add the sausage and tomatoes and cook for 4 minutes or until the sausage is golden.

Place the eggs, milk, sour cream, pepper and parsley in a bowl and whisk to combine. Reduce the heat to low and pour the egg mixture over the leek mixture in the pan. Sprinkle with the cheese and cook for 8 minutes or until the mixture is almost set. Place the frittata under a hot preheated griller (broiler) and grill until golden.

To make eggplant purée, peel and cut the eggplants into chunks and place them in a colander. Sprinkle with sea salt and allow to drain for 5 minutes. Rinse the eggplant in plenty of water and place in a saucepan of boiling water. Add the lemon juice and allow to simmer for 8 minutes or until the eggplant is soft. Drain the eggplant well and place in a food processor or blender with the garlic, cumin and butter and process until smooth. Add enough cream to thin to a soft purée. Return to the saucepan and heat gently until heated through.

To serve, cut the frittata into wedges and place on serving plates. Top with a generous spoonful of eggplant purée.

SERVES 4

EGGPLANT AND CASHEW NUT DIP

INGREDIENTS

1 eggplant (aubergine)

½ cup (125 g/4 oz) sour cream

1 spring onion (scallion), chopped

½ cup (75 g/2½ oz) roasted unsalted cashew nuts

⅓ cup (90 mL/3 fl oz) vegetable stock

1 teaspoon ground cumin

1 tablespoon fresh coriander (cilantro) leaves

extra cashew nuts

Place the eggplant on a baking sheet and bake in a preheated oven at 180°C (355°F) for 35 minutes or until soft. Scoop out the flesh from the skin and place in a food processor or blender with the sour cream, spring onion, cashew nuts, stock, cumin and coriander leaves and process until smooth. Transfer the mixture to a saucepan and simmer for 8 minutes or until the mixture has thickened.

To serve, place the dip in a bowl and sprinkle with extra cashew nuts. Serve warm with lavosh bread.

SERVES 4–6

EGGPLANT SANDWICHES

Cut the eggplant into 1 cm (⅓ in) thick slices. Place the slices in a colander, sprinkle with the sea salt, allow to drain for 10 minutes, rinse in plenty of water and pat dry with absorbent kitchen paper.

Place the capsicums under a hot preheated griller (broiler), skin sides up and grill until the skins have blistered and blackened. Place in a plastic bag and seal. Allow to stand for 5 minutes to steam the skins from the capsicums. Peel the skins from them and slice thinly.

Heat the oil in a frying pan or skillet over a medium heat until hot. Add the eggplant, a few pieces at a time, and cook for 2 minutes each side or until golden and crisp, then drain on absorbent kitchen paper.

To make basil mayonnaise, place the ingredients in a bowl and mix well to combine.

To assemble, place a few eggplant slices on each serving plate. Top with the capsicums, feta cheese, olives, capers and sun-dried tomatoes. Drizzle with basil mayonnaise and top each sandwich with the remaining eggplant. Serve immediately with toasted walnut bread.

SERVES 4–6

INGREDIENTS

2 eggplants (aubergines)

sea salt

2 red capsicums (sweet peppers), seeded and quartered

oil for shallow frying

340 g (11 oz) marinated feta cheese, roughly chopped

1 cup (155 g/5 oz) pitted marinated olives

2 tablespoons baby capers, rinsed

8 sun-dried tomatoes, sliced

Basil Mayonnaise

3 tablespoons chopped fresh basil leaves

1 tablespoon balsamic vinegar

½ cup whole egg mayonnaise (page 169)

cracked black pepper

PARCHMENT BAKED EGGPLANTS

Slice the eggplants into quarters lengthwise then place in a colander, sprinkle with the sea salt and allow to drain for 10 minutes. Rinse the eggplants in plenty of water and pat dry with absorbent kitchen paper.

Place each eggplant on a doubled square of baking parchment. Top each eggplant with tomatoes then a sprinkling of olive oil, rosemary, garlic, lemon juice, olives and pepper.

Gather the parchment edges and fold tightly to seal. Place on a baking sheet and bake in a preheated oven at 200°C (390°F) for 35–40 minutes or until the eggplant flesh is soft.

To serve, slightly open the parchment packages to let out steam and place on serving plates. Serve as a first course with pita bread.

SERVES 4

INGREDIENTS

2 eggplants (aubergines)

sea salt

4 egg-shaped (Roma/plum) tomatoes, halved

2 tablespoons olive oil

4 small rosemary sprigs

2 garlic cloves, thinly sliced

2 tablespoons lemon juice

⅔ cup (90 g/3 oz) Niçoise olives

cracked black pepper

baking parchment

Eggplant ravioli and Eggplant and pistachio pesto pizzas.

EGGPLANT RAVIOLI

Slice the eggplants very thinly, place in a colander and sprinkle with the sea salt. Allow to drain for 5 minutes then rinse in plenty of water and pat dry. Place the eggplant slices a few at a time in a saucepan of simmering water and cook for 1 minute. Drain and cool.

To make filling, place the ingredients in a bowl and mix to combine. Place a small spoonful of filling in the middle of each eggplant slice. Fold in half and secure with a toothpick (wooden pick).

Heat the oil in a frying pan or skillet over a high heat. Cook the eggplant ravioli a few at a time for 2–3 minutes each side or until they are golden. Keep warm. To make tomato salsa, place the ingredients in a bowl and mix to combine.

To serve, place the eggplant ravioli on serving plates and serve with a pile of tomato salsa.

SERVES 4–6

INGREDIENTS

2 small eggplants (aubergines)
sea salt
oil for shallow frying

Filling
185 g (6 oz) ricotta cheese
1 tablespoon chopped thyme leaves
1 fresh red chilli pepper, chopped
1 teaspoon toasted cumin seeds

Tomato Salsa
2 vine-ripened tomatoes, chopped
½ red onion, chopped
⅓ cup (60 g/2 oz) pitted olives, chopped
3 tablespoons chopped rocket (arugula) leaves
2 teaspoons soft brown sugar
2 tablespoons balsamic vinegar
cracked black pepper

EGGPLANT AND PISTACHIO PESTO PIZZAS

Place the eggplant in a colander, sprinkle with sea salt and allow to drain for 5 minutes. Rinse the eggplant in plenty of water and pat dry with absorbent kitchen paper. Heat the oil in a frying pan or skillet over a high heat. Add the eggplant, a few pieces at a time, and cook for 2 minutes each side or until golden. Set aside. Add the zucchini to the frying pan and cook, stirring, for 4 minutes or until soft.

To make pistachio pesto, place the pistachio nuts, mint and basil leaves, garlic and Parmesan cheese in a food processor or blender and process until finely chopped. Gradually add the oil while the motor is running and process to a smooth paste.

Divide the dough into six equal portions and roll out onto a lightly floured surface until dough is 4 mm (⅙ in) thick. Spread the dough rounds with the pesto and top with the eggplant, zucchini and cherry tomatoes. Sprinkle with Parmesan cheese and place on baking sheets.

Bake in a preheated oven at 200°C (390°F) for 25 minutes or until the crusts are crisp and golden. Serve pizzas with a green leaf salad.

SERVES 4–6

INGREDIENTS

1 quantity pizza dough (page 170)

Topping
2 eggplants (aubergines), thinly sliced
sea salt
2 tablespoons olive oil
1 zucchini (courgette), thinly sliced
125 g (4 oz) cherry tomatoes
¾ cup (90 g/3 oz) grated Parmesan cheese

Pistachio Pesto
⅓ cup (45 g/1½ oz) pistachio nuts
½ cup (30 g/1 oz) fresh mint leaves
½ cup (30 g/1 oz) fresh basil leaves
2 garlic cloves, crushed
¼ cup (30 g/1 oz) grated Parmesan, extra
3 tablespoons olive oil

CHAR-GRILLED VEAL, EGGPLANT PANCAKES

INGREDIENTS

4 veal steaks
1 tablespoon oil
2 tablespoons lemon juice
2 tablespoons chopped fresh chervil leaves
cracked black pepper
pinch chilli flakes

Eggplant Pancakes
1 eggplant (aubergine), finely chopped
sea salt
1 tablespoon oil, extra
1 cup (125 g/4 oz) self-raising flour
½ teaspoon baking powder
1¼ cups (310 mL/10 fl oz) milk
1 egg, lightly beaten
2 tablespoons pesto (page 169)
45 g (1½ oz) butter, melted

Trim the veal of any fat and place in a shallow bowl. Combine the oil, lemon juice, chervil leaves, pepper and chilli flakes and pour over the veal. Allow to marinate for 20 minutes.

To make eggplant pancakes, place the eggplant in a colander, sprinkle with sea salt and allow to drain for 5 minutes. Rinse the eggplant in plenty of water and dry with absorbent kitchen paper. Heat the oil in a frying pan or skillet over a high heat. Add the eggplant and cook, stirring, for 6 minutes or until the eggplant is well browned. Set aside to cool.

Place the flour and baking powder in a bowl. Whisk in the milk, egg, pesto and butter and continue whisking until smooth. Fold in the eggplant. Cook spoonfuls of the mixture in a greased frying pan over a medium heat for 2 minutes each side or until puffed and golden. Keep warm. Drain the veal and cook it on a very hot char-grill or barbecue for 1–2 minutes each side or to your liking.

To serve, place the pancakes on serving plates. Slice the veal and pile it on top of the pancakes then finish with a spoonful of hummus.

SERVES 4

MARINATED EGGPLANT SALAD

INGREDIENTS

2 eggplants (aubergines), sliced
sea salt
2 tablespoons olive oil
1 garlic clove, crushed
2 tablespoons fresh oregano leaves
2 tablespoons fresh basil leaves
1 tablespoon grated orange rind
⅓ cup (90 mL/3 fl oz) balsamic vinegar
2 tablespoons hazelnut oil
4 figs, sliced
salad greens
cracked black pepper

Place the eggplant in a colander and sprinkle with the sea salt. Allow to stand for 5 minutes then rinse in plenty of water and pat dry with absorbent kitchen paper. Brush the eggplant slices lightly with olive oil and cook under a hot preheated griller (broiler) for 2 minutes each side or until golden. Place the garlic, oregano and basil leaves, orange rind, balsamic vinegar and hazelnut oil in a food processor or blender and process until smooth.

Put the eggplant slices in a bowl and pour over the marinade. Cover and refrigerate for at least 1 hour or preferably overnight.

To serve, place eggplant slices on serving plates with slices of fig and salad greens. Sprinkle with pepper and spoon over the remaining marinade. Serve with warm herbed bread.

SERVES 4

MOROCCAN COUS COUS

This is a great and flavoursome method of steaming cous cous which is enhanced by the spiced vegetables.

Place the cous cous in a bowl and pour over the boiling water. Stand for 5 minutes. Stir with a fork to separate the grains and set aside. Place the eggplant in a colander, sprinkle with sea salt and drain for 5 minutes then rinse the eggplant in plenty of water. Drain again and pat dry with absorbent kitchen paper.

Heat the oil in a saucepan over a high heat. Add the onions and cook for 3 minutes or until the onions are soft and golden. Add the saffron threads, cinnamon, ginger and cumin and cook for 1 minute. Add the eggplant, capsicum, zucchinis, chickpeas, lemon rind, tomato puree and stock to the saucepan and reduce the heat to a simmer.

Place the cous cous in a muslin lined colander or steamer and place over the saucepan of simmering vegetables. Allow to simmer for 15 minutes then remove the colander from the saucepan and toss the butter and currants through the cous cous. Serve the cous cous with the spiced vegetables.

SERVES 4

INGREDIENTS

1½ cups (310 g/10 oz) cous cous
1 cup (250 mL/8 fl oz) boiling water
1 eggplant (aubergine), chopped
sea salt
1 tablespoon olive oil
2 onions, chopped
4 saffron threads
½ teaspoon ground cinnamon
2 teaspoons grated fresh ginger
1 teaspoon ground cumin
1 green capsicum (sweet pepper), chopped
2 zucchinis (courgettes), chopped
1 cup (225 g/7 oz) cooked chickpeas (garbanzo beans)
2 teaspoons grated lemon rind
1½ cups (375 mL/12 fl oz) tomato purée (passata)
½ cup (125 mL/4 fl oz) vegetable stock
60 g (2 oz) butter, chopped
⅓ cup (60 g/2 oz) currants

SLOW GRILLED EGGPLANT

Prick the eggplants once with a skewer and place over glowing hot coals or on a barbecue, far enough away from the heat to allow the eggplants to cook slowly. Turn the eggplants as their skins blacken. When the eggplants are blackened all over and are soft, remove them from the heat.

Peel the top section of skin away from the eggplants to expose the flesh and place on individual serving plates. Melt the butter in a saucepan over a medium heat. Add the garlic, thyme leaves, lemon juice, coriander and pepper and simmer until the butter is golden.

To serve, cut slits in the flesh of the eggplants to allow the flavoured butter to flow through the flesh. Pour the flavoured butter over the eggplants and serve with grilled meats or garlic smothered lamb (page 92).

SERVES 4

INGREDIENTS

4 small eggplants (aubergines)
90 g (3 oz) butter
2 garlic cloves, crushed
1 tablespoon fresh lemon thyme leaves
2 teaspoons lemon juice
1 teaspoon ground coriander
cracked black pepper

Herbs.

CHAPTER 11

Herbs

SAGE RISOTTO CAKES

INGREDIENTS

1 tablespoon butter

4 golden shallots, chopped

1 tablespoon chopped fresh sage leaves

1 chorizo or spicy sausage, chopped

1 cup (225 g/7 oz) Arborio rice

1½ cups (375 mL/12 fl oz) chicken or vegetable stock

⅓ cup (90 mL/3 fl oz) dry white wine

1 egg, lightly beaten

1 cup (60 g/2 oz) fresh breadcrumbs

1 tablespoon oil

Melt the butter in a saucepan over a high heat. Add the shallots, sage leaves and sausage and sauté for 5 minutes or until golden. Remove the sausage mixture from the pan leaving the juices behind.

Place the rice in a saucepan with the remaining juices and cook over a high heat, stirring, for 4 minutes or until the grains are translucent. Place the stock and wine in a separate saucepan over a high heat and heat until boiling. Keep the stock mixture hot. Add the stock mixture to the rice 1 cup at a time, stirring constantly, until the stock has been absorbed. Continue adding the stock until it is all used and the rice is creamy and soft. Remove from the heat, mix through the sausage mixture and allow to cool.

When the mixture is cool, stir in the egg and breadcrumbs. Shape a few tablespoons of the mixture into a small cake and repeat with the remaining mixture. Heat the oil in a frying pan or skillet over a medium heat and add the risotto cakes to the pan. Cook for 2 minutes each side or until golden and crisp. Serve warm with drinks.

SERVES 4–6

STEAMED HERB VEGETABLES WITH WONTONS

INGREDIENTS

2 dill sprigs

2 basil sprigs

3 lemon thyme sprigs

2 sage sprigs

12 baby carrots

12 broccoli florets

12 baby zucchinis (courgettes)

12 baby corn cobs

6 slices red capsicum (sweet pepper)

Wontons

375 g (12 oz) chicken mince

2 tablespoons chopped fresh coriander (cilantro) leaves

½ teaspoon ground cinnamon

1 fresh red chilli pepper, chopped

1 egg white

24 wonton wrappers

Line the base of a large bamboo steamer with the dill, basil, lemon thyme and sage. Arrange the carrots, broccoli, zucchinis, corn cobs and capsicum on top of the herbs. To make wontons, place the chicken mince, coriander leaves, cinnamon, chilli pepper and egg white in a bowl and beat well. Place a tablespoon of mixture on each wonton wrapper. Gather the edges of the wonton together and twist to seal. Place wontons in a large, greased bamboo steamer.

Place the wonton steamer on top of the vegetable steamer and cover with a steamer lid. Place steamers over a wok or saucepan of simmering water and allow to steam for 8 minutes or until the vegetables are cooked and the wontons are tender.

To serve, place steamers in the middle of the table and serve with individual bowls of rice and sweet chilli and soy sauce.

SERVES 4

BASIL, FETA AND TOMATO PIZZAS

Divide the pizza dough into four equal portions and roll out on a lightly floured surface until 7 mm (¼ in) thick. Place on greased baking sheets and set aside.

To make topping, place the tomatoes, cut side up, on a baking sheet and drizzle with a little oil and pepper. Bake in a preheated oven at 160°C (315°F) for 20 minutes or until soft.

Melt the butter in a frying pan or skillet over a high heat. Add the onions and cook for 3 minutes or until golden. Reduce the heat, add the anchovies and cook for 5 minutes or until the onions are very soft. Spread the pizzas with the onion mixture and top with the tomatoes, basil leaves and feta cheese. Sprinkle with the peppercorns and bake in preheated oven at 200°C (390°F) for 25 minutes or until the bases are golden and the topping is hot.

SERVES 4

INGREDIENTS

1 quantity pizza dough (page 170)

Topping

8 egg-shaped (Roma/plum) tomatoes, halved

olive oil

cracked black pepper

1 tablespoon butter

3 onions, sliced

4 anchovies, rinsed and chopped

4 tablespoons fresh basil leaves

435 g (14 oz) feta cheese, chopped

1 tablespoon green peppercorns, lightly crushed

SALMON CAKES, SORREL CREAM

Remove any visible bones from the salmon. Add the salmon and bouquet garni to a frying pan or skillet of simmering water and poach the salmon for 5 minutes or until the flesh is tender. Remove from the frying pan and drain on absorbent kitchen paper. Remove the salmon from its skin and flake into a bowl, removing the bones as you go. Add the chives, thyme leaves, egg white, breadcrumbs, lemon juice and pepper to the salmon and mix to combine. With floured hands, shape the salmon mixture into small cakes. Allow the cakes to stand, covered, in the refrigerator for 1 hour.

To make sorrel cream, melt the butter in a saucepan over a medium heat. Add the spring onions and sorrel and sauté for 2 minutes. Add the cream, stock and mustard and simmer for 15 minutes or until the liquid has reduced and thickened slightly.

Place the sorrel mixture into a blender or food processor and process until smooth. Return to the saucepan and keep warm.

To cook salmon cakes, heat the oil in a frying pan over a medium heat. Cook the salmon cakes a few at a time for 1–2 minutes each side or until golden. Serve with small pots of sorrel cream and sorrel.

SERVES 6

INGREDIENTS

750 g (1½ lbs) salmon fillet

bouquet garni

2 tablespoons chopped fresh chives

2 tablespoons chopped fresh lemon thyme

1 egg white

½ cup (30 g/1 oz) fresh breadcrumbs

2 tablespoons lemon juice

cracked black pepper

1 tablespoon oil

Sorrel Cream

1 tablespoon butter

2 spring onions (scallions), chopped

90 g (3 oz) young sorrel

1 cup (250 mL/8 fl oz) light (single) cream

½ cup (125 mL/4 fl oz) fish stock

2 teaspoons Dijon mustard

GOAT'S CHEESE SALAD WITH HERB ASH

INGREDIENTS

mixed salad leaves

4 small goat's cheese rounds

pomegranate molasses

Herb Ash

6 fresh sage leaves

2 rosemary sprigs

2 thyme sprigs

2 marjoram sprigs

To make herb ash, place the herbs in a saucepan with a tight-fitting lid and cook over a medium heat without lifting the lid for 20 minutes. Still without lifting the lid, allow to stand for 30 minutes.

Place the herb ashes in a mortar and pestle, food processor or blender and process to a powder. Sprinkle over the goat's cheese rounds, cover and refrigerate for at least 2 hours or preferably overnight.

To serve, arrange the salad leaves on serving plates, top with a round of goat's cheese and sprinkle with pomegranate molasses.

SERVES 4

LIME REEF FISH WITH THAI POTATO CAKES

INGREDIENTS

6 reef fish fillets

3 tablespoons lime juice

2 teaspoons grated lime rind

1 garlic clove, crushed

⅓ cup (45 g/1½ oz) pine nuts

1 teaspoon cumin seeds

1 tablespoon chopped fresh parsley

2 tablespoons olive oil

Potato Cakes

3 starchy potatoes, peeled

1 tablespoon grated fresh ginger

½ lemon grass stalk, finely chopped

1 fresh red chilli pepper, chopped

1 tablespoon fresh coriander (cilantro) leaves

1 egg white, lightly beaten

2 tablespoons plain (all-purpose) flour

oil for shallow frying

I like fish with something crunchy. These potato cakes are also great served with a chunky salsa to go with drinks.

Remove any visible bones and place the fish on an oiled sheet of aluminium kitchen foil on a baking sheet.

Place the lime juice and rind, garlic, pine nuts, cumin seeds, parsley and olive oil in a food processor or blender and process until the mixture is smooth. Brush well over both sides of the fish.

To make potato cakes, grate the potatoes finely into a bowl. Add the ginger, lemon grass stalk, chilli pepper, coriander leaves, egg white and flour and mix well. Heat the oil in a frying pan or skillet until hot. Place spoonfuls of the mixture into the oil and flatten with a spatula. Cook for 2–3 minutes each side or until the potato cakes are crisp and golden. Drain on absorbent kitchen paper and keep warm.

Bake the fish in a preheated oven at 180°C (355°F) for 30 minutes or until the fish flakes when pressed with a fork.

To serve, place the potato cakes on serving plates and top with the fish, serve immediately with a mixed tomato salad.

SERVES 6

Goat's cheese salad with herb ash.

ROSEMARY CHICKEN SKEWERS

INGREDIENTS

4 chicken breast fillets

2 tablespoons lime juice

1 tablespoon chopped fresh tarragon leaves

2 fresh red chilli peppers, seeded and chopped

1 teaspoon cumin seeds

1 tablespoon walnut oil

8 sturdy rosemary stalks

Slice the chicken breast fillets in half length-wise. Combine the lime juice, tarragon leaves, chilli peppers, cumin seeds and oil in a bowl.

Make a hole through each chicken piece using a thick metal skewer. Thread the rosemary through the hole to make a skewer. Brush the chicken with the marinade mixture and cook on a hot preheated barbecue or a preheated griller (broiler) for 3–4 minutes each side or until golden and cooked through.

Serve the chicken skewers straight from the barbecue with a salad of tomatoes and mozzarella cheese.

SERVES 4

LAMB WITH SAGE AND ROSEMARY SOUFFLES

INGREDIENTS

1.5 kg (3lbs) boned loin of lamb

Stuffing

2 cups (125 g/4 oz) fresh breadcrumbs

1 tablespoon chopped fresh rosemary

2 tablespoons seeded mustard

2 eggs, lightly beaten

½ cup (60 g/2 oz) roasted cashew nuts, chopped

Sage and Rosemary Soufflés

2 tablespoons butter

1 garlic clove, crushed

2 tablespoons plain (all-purpose) flour

1 cup (250 mL/8 fl oz) milk

4 eggs, separated

1 tablespoon finely chopped fresh rosemary leaves

1 tablespoon chopped fresh sage leaves

½ cup (60 g/2 oz) grated aged cheddar cheese

cracked black pepper

To make stuffing, place the ingredients in a bowl and mix to combine. Press the stuffing along the lamb, roll and tie up with string.

Place the lamb in a baking pan and bake in a preheated oven at 200°C (390°F) for 1 hour or until cooked to your liking.

To make soufflés, melt the butter in a saucepan over a medium heat. Add the garlic and sauté for 1 minute. Stir in the flour and continue stirring while cooking for 1 minute. Remove from the heat and whisk in the milk. Return to the heat and stir until the mixture boils and thickens. Remove from the heat and allow to cool.

Mix in the egg yolks, rosemary leaves, sage leaves, cheddar cheese and pepper and set aside. Place the egg whites in a bowl and beat until stiff peaks form. Fold the egg whites through the herb mixture and pour into four greased 1 cup (250 mL/8 fl oz) capacity ramekins. About 15 minutes before the end of the lamb's cooking time, place the soufflés in the oven and bake for 15–18 minutes or until golden.

To serve, carve the lamb and place it on serving plates with a sage and rosemary soufflé. Serve with baby green peas tossed in fresh mint and butter.

SERVES 4

SMOKED HERB CHICKEN WITH FILLED BABY EGGPLANTS

This recipe is well worth lighting the barbecue for. Fragrant smoked chicken with smoky flavoured eggplant, soft tomatoes and melted mozzarella cheese.

Trim the chicken of any excess fat, rinse the cavity and dry with absorbent kitchen paper. Place the cinnamon stick, star anise pod, bay leaves, lemon thyme sprigs and garlic chives in the cavity and truss the chicken. Brush with oil and place in a baking pan.

Place the chicken in a covered barbecue heated until the coals have turned white. Cover the barbecue and cook for 15 minutes.

Make three length-wise slits in each eggplant, leaving the stem end intact. Place the eggplants in a baking pan. Fill the slits in each eggplant with slices of tomato and basil leaves. Sprinkle with the mozzarella cheese and pepper and place in the barbecue with the chicken.

Cook the chicken and eggplant for a further 10 minutes. Soak the wood chips in water for 10 minutes then place them on the hot coals. Place the cover back onto the barbecue and cook for a further 10–15 minutes or until the chicken is cooked, the eggplant is soft and the cheese is golden.

To serve, cut the chicken into pieces and serve with a baby eggplant.

SERVES 4

INGREDIENTS

1.5 kg (3 lbs) chicken
1 cinnamon stick
2 star anise pods
3 bay leaves
2 lemon thyme sprigs
4 garlic chives, halved
oil
fragrant wood chips

Filled Baby Eggplants
4 baby eggplants (aubergines)
4 egg-shaped (Roma/plum) tomatoes, sliced
2 tablespoons fresh basil leaves
1 cup (125 g/4 oz) grated mozzarella cheese
cracked black pepper

VEAL WITH OREGANO AND CREAMY POLENTA

INGREDIENTS

1 tablespoon butter

1 tablespoon oil

2 tablespoons fresh oregano leaves

4 thick veal scotch fillet steaks

½ cup (125 mL/4 fl oz) dry white wine

½ cup (125 mL/4 fl oz) veal or chicken stock

Creamy Polenta

4 cups (1 litre/1¾ imp. pints) water

1½ cups (375 mL/12 fl oz) beef or vegetable stock

1 cup (185 g/6 oz) polenta (cornmeal)

30 g (1 oz) butter

½ cup (125 g/4 oz) sour cream

⅓ cup (45 g/1½ oz) grated Parmesan cheese

cracked black pepper

To make creamy polenta, heat the water and stock in a saucepan over a high heat until it comes to the boil. Gradually add the polenta, stirring continually. Reduce the heat to medium and cook for 40 minutes or until the polenta leaves the sides of the saucepan.

To cook veal, heat the butter and oil in a frying pan or skillet over a high heat. Add the oregano leaves and cook for 1 minute or until crisp. Remove the oregano leaves from the pan with a slotted spoon and set aside. Place the veal in the pan and sear on both sides for 30 seconds. Meanwhile, cook the veal.

Place the veal on a baking sheet and cover with aluminium kitchen foil. Place in a preheated oven at 140°C (275°F) for 8–10 minutes or until cooked to your liking. Add the wine and stock to the veal juices in the pan and cook over a medium heat for 5 minutes or until the liquid has reduced by half. To finish the polenta, add the butter, sour cream, Parmesan cheese and pepper to the saucepan and cook, stirring, for 4 minutes or until heated through.

To serve, place piles of creamy polenta on serving plates and top with the veal. Pour pan juices over veal and top with oregano leaves.

SERVES 4

HERB WRAPPED BARBECUE TROUT

INGREDIENTS

4 small river (rainbow) trout

2 limes, sliced

1 garlic clove, sliced

8 bay leaves

8 dill sprigs

8 thyme sprigs

8 marjoram sprigs

3 tablespoons olive oil

cracked black pepper

Lime and Dill Butter

90 g (3 oz) butter, softened

2 teaspoons grated lime rind

1 tablespoon lime juice

½ teaspoon ground cumin

1 tablespoon chopped fresh dill

Clean the trout in plenty of water and pat dry with absorbent kitchen paper. Place the lime and garlic slices in the fish cavity. Divide the herbs into eight separate bundles, place a bundle on the side of each fish and tie on with string.

Place the trout on a preheated barbecue plate and sprinkle with the olive oil and pepper. Cook for 2–4 minutes each side or until tender.

To make lime and dill butter, place the butter, lime rind and juice, cumin and dill in a bowl and mix to combine.

Serve the trout with barbecued potato slices and generous dollops of lime and dill butter.

SERVES 4

Veal with oregano and creamy polenta.

LAVENDER BRULEE WITH SUGAR COOKIES

INGREDIENTS

10 lavender stems
1 small piece lemon rind
3 cups (750 mL/24 fl oz) light (single) cream
8 egg yolks
2 tablespoons caster (superfine) sugar
white granulated sugar for topping
2 lavender flowers, chopped

Sugar Cookies
60 g (2 oz) butter
½ teaspoon vanilla extract
½ cup (125 g/4 oz) white granulated sugar
1 egg
1 tablespoon chopped lavender flowers
¾ cup (90 g/3 oz) self-raising flour
icing (confectioners') sugar

Lightly scented lavender crème brûlée accompanied by crisp sugar cookies. Crème with crunch!

To make brûlée, wash the lavender well and place it in a saucepan with the lemon rind and cream. Place over a low heat and allow the mixture to heat until almost boiling. Remove from the heat and allow to stand for 10 minutes. Strain the cream mixture through a fine sieve.

Place the egg yolks and caster sugar in a bowl and beat until thick and creamy. Gradually add the cream mixture and beat well. Return the mixture to the saucepan, place over a low heat and stir until the mixture thickens slightly.

Pour the mixture into six ½ cup (125 mL/4 fl oz) capacity ramekins or pots and refrigerate for 3 hours or until set.

To make sugar cookies, place the butter, vanilla extract and sugar in a bowl and beat until light and creamy. Add the egg and beat well. Mix in the lavender flowers and flour. Place teaspoons of the mixture onto greased baking sheets and place in a preheated oven at 190°C (375°F) for 8 minutes or until the edges are golden. Cool on wire racks and dust with icing sugar.

To serve, place the brûlées in a baking pan and pack ice around the ramekins. Sprinkle the tops of the ramekins with the sugar and lavender flowers. Place under a hot preheated griller (broiler) and cook for 1–2 minutes or until the sugar has melted and is golden. Stand for 3 minutes then serve on individual serving plates with a small stack of sugar cookies.

SERVES 6

ROSE GERANIUM CAKE

Wrap the butter in the rose geranium leaves, cover and place in the refrigerator for 5 hours or preferably overnight. Remove the leaves from the butter and roughly chop the butter. Place it in a bowl with the vanilla extract and caster sugar and beat until light and creamy.

Gradually add the eggs and beat well. Fold through the combined flours and pour the mixture into a greased 23 cm (9½ in) round cake tin. Bake in a preheated oven at 180°C (355°F) for 1 hour or until cooked through. Let the cake stand in the tin for 5 minutes and then turn it out to cool on a wire rack.

To make frosting, place the cream and geranium leaves in a small saucepan over a medium heat. Allow the mixture to come to the boil. Remove from the heat and refrigerate. Remove the leaves and beat the cold cream until soft peaks form. Fold through the icing sugar.

To serve, spread the cake with the frosting and decorate with rose geranium leaves and flowers. Serve with a selection of flower teas.

SERVES 8

INGREDIENTS

250 g (8 oz) butter

8 rose geranium leaves

½ teaspoon vanilla extract

1 cup (225 g/7 oz) caster (superfine) sugar

4 eggs

½ cup (60 g/2 oz) self-raising flour

1 cup (125 g/4 oz) plain (all-purpose) flour

Frosting

1 cup (250 mL/8 fl oz) light (single) cream

2 rose geranium leaves

2 teaspoons icing (confectioners') sugar

PANCAKES WITH LEMON VERBENA SYRUP

To make lemon verbena syrup, place the maple syrup in a saucepan over a low heat. Add the lemon verbena sprigs and heat for 5 minutes. Remove from the heat and allow to stand until cold. Remove the lemon verbena sprigs and store the syrup in a sterilised jar or bottle in the refrigerator.

To make pancakes, mix the flour and caster sugar in a bowl and make a well in the centre. Add the buttermilk, egg and melted butter and mix until smooth. Pour rounds of the mixture into a greased frying pan or skillet and cook over a medium heat for 1–2 minutes each side or until golden brown.

Serve the pancakes in small stacks drizzled with lemon verbena syrup and accompanied by a scoop of vanilla bean ice cream.

SERVES 4–6

INGREDIENTS

Pancakes

2 cups (250 g/8 oz) self-raising flour

3 tablespoons caster (superfine) sugar

1¾ cups (435 mL/14 fl oz) buttermilk

1 egg, lightly beaten

2 tablespoons butter, melted

Lemon Verbena Syrup

2 cups (500 mL/16 fl oz) maple syrup

6 lemon verbena sprigs

Lemons, limes and tangelos.

CHAPTER 12

Lemons, limes and tangelos

MOROCCAN LAMB WITH LEMON COUS COUS

INGREDIENTS

1 onion, chopped
2 garlic cloves, crushed
2 teaspoons cumin seeds
2 teaspoons coriander seeds
2 tablespoons fresh mint leaves
2 teaspoons harissa (page 53)
2 teaspoons chopped preserved lemons
leg lamb (approx 1.5 kg/3 lbs)

Lemon Cous Cous

1½ cups (310 g/10 oz) cous cous
2 cups (500 mL/16 fl oz) boiling water
1 tablespoon olive oil
2 onions, sliced
1 tablespoon shredded lemon rind
1 tablespoon lemon juice
½ cup (75 g/2½ oz) Niçoise olives

Place the onion, garlic, cumin seeds, coriander seeds, mint leaves, harissa and preserved lemons in a food processor or blender and process until smooth. Spread the mixture evenly over the lamb and then place the lamb on a wire rack in a baking pan. Pour water in the base of the baking pan until it almost reaches the baking rack. Bake the lamb in a preheated oven at 190°C (375°F) for 1 hour or until the lamb is cooked to your liking.

To make lemon cous cous, place the cous cous and boiling water in a bowl, cover and allow to stand for 5 minutes. Heat the oil in a frying pan over a medium heat, add the onions and cook for 5–7 minutes or until the onions are brown and crisp. Add the lemon rind, lemon juice, cous cous and olives and cook, stirring, for 2 minutes.

To serve, slice the lamb and place it on serving plates with lemon cous cous and a spoonful of harissa (page 53) or chilli jam (page 47).

SERVES 4

POACHED OCEAN TROUT WITH LIME HOLLANDAISE

INGREDIENTS

2 cups (500 mL/16 fl oz) water
1 teaspoon black peppercorns
2 lime wedges
2 lemon thyme sprigs
2 x 405 g (13 oz) ocean trout fillets

Lime Hollandaise

185 g (6 oz) butter
3 tablespoons water
3 egg yolks
2 tablespoons lime juice
1 teaspoon finely grated lime rind

To poach the trout, place the water, peppercorns, lime wedges and lemon thyme in a large frying pan or skillet over a high heat. Bring to the boil then reduce the temperature so that the liquid simmers. Add the trout fillets and poach them for 2 minutes each side or until the trout is tender. Remove the trout with a slotted spoon.

To make lime hollandaise, melt the butter in a small saucepan over a low heat. Allow the butter to cool slightly. Place the water and egg yolks in a small, heavy based saucepan and whisk until well combined. Place the saucepan over a very low heat and whisk the egg mixture until it is thick. Remove from the heat and gradually pour in the butter, whisking well. Whisk in the lime juice and rind. To serve, cut the trout fillets in half, spoon over the lime hollandaise and serve with asparagus and salt rosemary baked potatoes (page 72).

SERVES 4

LIME AND LEMON GRASS CHICKEN

An Asian-inspired recipe that is pungent with flavour.

Trim the chicken of fat and cut the fillets into two. Heat the oil in a large frying pan, skillet or a wok over a high heat. Add the chicken and cook for 4 minutes or until the chicken is golden brown on both sides. Remove from the pan and set aside.

Add the lime rind, chilli peppers, lime leaves, lemon grass stalks, brown sugar, galangal, cumin, lime juice and tamarind paste to the pan and cook, stirring, for 2 minutes.

Return the chicken to the pan and then add the coconut cream and stock. Allow to simmer for 30 minutes or until the chicken is tender and the sauce has thickened slightly. The finished dish will still be quite liquid. Serve the chicken with piles of steamed jasmine rice and pawpaw chutney or with a combination of chopped mango, fresh mint and plain yoghurt.

SERVES 4

INGREDIENTS

6 chicken thigh fillets
2 teaspoons sesame oil
2 teaspoons grated lime rind
2 fresh red chilli peppers, chopped
2 kaffir lime leaves, sliced
2 lemon grass stalks, chopped
1 tablespoon palm or brown sugar
2 teaspoons grated galangal
2 teaspoons ground cumin
1 tablespoon lime juice
2 teaspoons tamarind paste
1 cup (250 mL/8 fl oz) coconut cream
1 cup (250 mL/8 fl oz) chicken stock

LEMON POPPYSEED MUFFINS

With a cup of strong coffee and a warm muffin with melting whipped maple butter, breakfast never looked so good.

Sift the flour and baking powder into a bowl. Add the demerara sugar and stir to combine. Place the eggs, milk, sour cream, oil, lemon juice and rind and poppyseeds in another bowl and mix well to combine. Pour the liquid into the flour mixture and mix for 10 seconds or until just combined. Spoon the mixture into six greased 1 cup (250 mL/ 8 fl oz) capacity muffin pans (pans should be three-quarters full) and bake in a preheated oven at 180°C (355°F) for 25–30 minutes or until the muffins are cooked when tested with a skewer.

To make whipped maple butter, place the lemon rind, butter and maple syrup in a bowl and beat until light and fluffy. Refrigerate until required. Serve the muffins warm with whipped maple butter.

MAKES 6 LARGE MUFFINS

INGREDIENTS

1¾ cups (225 g/7 oz) self-raising flour
½ teaspoon baking powder
½ cup (125 g/4 oz) demerara sugar
2 eggs, lightly beaten
½ cup (125 mL/4 fl oz) milk
½ cup (125 g/4 oz) sour cream
3 tablespoons oil
2 tablespoons lemon juice
1 tablespoon grated lemon rind
¼ cup (45 g/1½ oz) poppyseeds

Whipped Maple Butter
2 teaspoons grated lemon rind
90 g (3 oz) butter
2 tablespoons maple syrup

Blood oranges in Sauternes.

BLOOD ORANGES IN SAUTERNES

A dessert with a glorious colour and a flavour to match.

Carefully peel the oranges, removing all the pith, and cut into quarters. Place the oranges and Sauternes in a bowl and allow to stand for 30 minutes. Drain the Sauternes into a saucepan with the sugar, cardamom pods and vanilla bean. Stir over a low heat until the sugar has dissolved. Increase the heat and allow to simmer for 2 minutes. Add the oranges and simmer for a further 3 minutes. Remove the cardamom pods and vanilla bean.

To serve, place the oranges on individual serving plates and top generously with syrup. Serve with a spoonful of heavy cream sprinkled with nutmeg.

SERVES 4

INGREDIENTS

3 blood oranges

1 cup (250 mL/8 fl oz) Sauternes

⅓ cup (90 g/3 oz) white granulated sugar

3 cardamom pods, bruised

1 vanilla bean, split

GRILLED ORANGE SABAYON WITH ALMOND CAKE

A partnership of light, grilled sabayon with rich, moist almond cake.

Place the butter and sugar in a bowl and beat until light and creamy. Add the egg yolks gradually and beat well. Fold the ground almonds through the butter mixture. Place the egg whites in another bowl and beat until stiff peaks form, gradually add the extra sugar and beat until glossy. Fold the egg whites through the almond mixture and pour into a greased 18 cm × 28 cm (7 in × 11 in) cake tin and bake in a preheated oven at 150°C (300°F) for 45 minutes or until the cake is cooked when tested with a skewer. Allow the cake to cool in the tin.

To make orange sabayon, place the ingredients in a heatproof bowl and whisk well. Place the bowl over a saucepan of simmering water and continue whisking until the sabayon is thick.

To serve, cut the cake into squares and place it on dessert plates. Pour the sabayon over the cake and place the plates under a hot griller (broiler) for 30 seconds or until golden. Serve.

SERVES 8

INGREDIENTS

125 g (4 oz) butter

3/4 cup (185 g/6 oz) white granulated sugar

4 eggs, separated

2½ cups (250 g/8 oz) ground almonds

¼ cup (60 g/2 oz) white granulated sugar, extra

Orange Sabayon

4 egg yolks

¼ cup (60 g/2 oz) white granulated sugar

½ cup (125 mL/4 fl oz) sweet white wine

2 teaspoons grated orange rind

KUMQUAT PANFORTE

INGREDIENTS

250 g (8 oz) kumquats

1 cup (250 mL/8 fl oz) Marsala

1½ cups (250 g/8 oz) soft brown sugar

¾ cup (185 mL/6 fl oz) honey

125 g (4 oz) dried apricots, chopped

125 g (4 oz) dried figs, chopped

200 g (6½ oz) roasted hazelnuts, chopped

200 g (6½ oz) roasted almonds, chopped

¾ cup (90 g/3 oz) plain (all-purpose) flour

⅓ cup (30 g/1 oz) cocoa powder

1 teaspoon ground cinnamon

icing (confectioners') sugar to dust

This recipe brings back memories of Sienna—perfect countryside, coffee, gelato and an astounding magnitude of panforte.

Slice the kumquats and place in a bowl with the Marsala. Allow to stand for at least 30 minutes. Place the kumquat mixture and brown sugar in a frying pan or skillet over a low heat and stir until the sugar has dissolved. Allow the mixture to slowly simmer for 20 minutes or until the kumquats are soft.

Place the kumquat mixture and the remaining ingredients in a bowl and mix to combine. Line a 28 cm × 18 cm (11 in × 7 in) cake tin with rice paper. Pour the mixture into the tin and bake in a preheated oven at 160°C (315°F) for 25–30 minutes or until firm. Allow the panforte to cool in the tin.

To serve the panforte, cut it into pieces, dust with icing sugar and serve with coffee and a dessert wine.

MAKES 32

MANDARIN CAKE WITH BUTTER SYRUP

INGREDIENTS

125 g (4 oz) butter

¾ cup (185 g/6 oz) caster (superfine) sugar

1½ tablespoons grated mandarin rind

2 eggs, lightly beaten

1½ cups (185g/6 oz) plain (all-purpose) flour

1½ teaspoons baking powder

½ cup (90 g/3 oz) thick plain yoghurt

¾ cup (185 mL/6 fl oz) mandarin juice

Butter Syrup

¾ cup (185 g/6 oz) white granulated sugar

½ cup (125 mL/4 fl oz) mandarin juice

2 tablespoons brandy or Sauternes

60 g (2 oz) butter

Place the butter, caster sugar and mandarin rind in a bowl and beat until light and creamy. Add the eggs gradually and beat well. Fold through the flour, baking powder, yoghurt and mandarin juice and continue folding until the ingredients are combined. Pour the mixture into a greased 20 cm (8 in) round cake tin and bake in a preheated oven at 180°C (355°F) for 40–50 minutes or until the cake is cooked when tested with a skewer.

To make butter syrup, place the sugar, mandarin juice and brandy in a saucepan over a low heat. Stir until the sugar has completely dissolved. Add the butter to the syrup and bring the mixture to a slow boil. Reduce the heat and allow the syrup to simmer for 3 minutes. Pour the hot syrup over the hot cake while it is still in the tin. Allow to stand for 5 minutes before removing the cake from the tin.

Serve each slice of cake with thick plain yoghurt or heavy cream.

SERVES 8

BURNT SUGAR TANGELO TART

To make pastry, place the butter, flour and icing sugar in a food processor and process until the mixture resembles fine breadcrumbs. Add enough water to form a smooth dough. Wrap in plastic wrap (cling film) and refrigerate for 30 minutes. Roll out the pastry on a lightly floured surface to fit a 25 cm (10 in) removable base tart tin. Line the pastry with nonstick baking parchment and fill with baking weights or rice. Bake in a preheated oven at 180°C (355°F) for 10 minutes, then remove the weights and parchment and bake for a further 5 minutes or until the pastry is golden.

To make filling, in a large bowl combine the sugar, eggs, cream and tangelo juice. Pour the mixture into the pastry case and bake at 180°C (355°F) for 45 minutes or until the filling is set. Allow to cool. Sprinkle the tart generously with extra caster sugar and place it under a hot preheated griller (broiler) for 2 minutes or until it is golden brown.

To serve, cut the tart into wedges and place on serving plates with a spoonful of vanilla bean ice cream and candied tangelo peel.

SERVES 8–10

INGREDIENTS

Pastry

125 g (4 oz) butter, chopped

2 cups (250 g/8 oz) plain (all-purpose) flour

2 tablespoons icing (confectioners') sugar

2–3 tablespoons iced water

Filling

1 cup (225 g/7 oz) caster (superfine) sugar

6 eggs

200 mL (6½ fl oz) light (double) cream

200 mL (6½ fl oz) tangelo juice

extra caster (superfine) sugar

TINY LIME AND LEMON MADELEINES

Subtle flavoured tiny madeleines are perfect for an afternoon tea party served with other small cakes and sweets.

Sift the flour and baking powder into a bowl and set aside. Place the eggs, caster sugar, lime and lemon rind in a bowl and beat until thick or until the mixture holds a ribbon trail. Fold the flour through the egg mixture in three batches. Fold in the butter with the last batch.

Place the mixture in the refrigerator for 10–15 minutes or until the butter hardens and the mixture thickens. Spoon it into greased and floured small madeleine tins and bake in a preheated oven at 200°C (390°F) for 5–7 minutes or until puffed and golden. Dust with icing sugar before serving.

MAKES 36

INGREDIENTS

½ cup (60 g/2 oz) plain (all-purpose) flour

⅓ teaspoon baking powder

2 eggs

½ cup (125 g/4 oz) caster (superfine) sugar

1 teaspoon grated lime rind

1 teaspoon grated lemon rind

60 g (2 oz) butter, melted

icing (confectioners') sugar

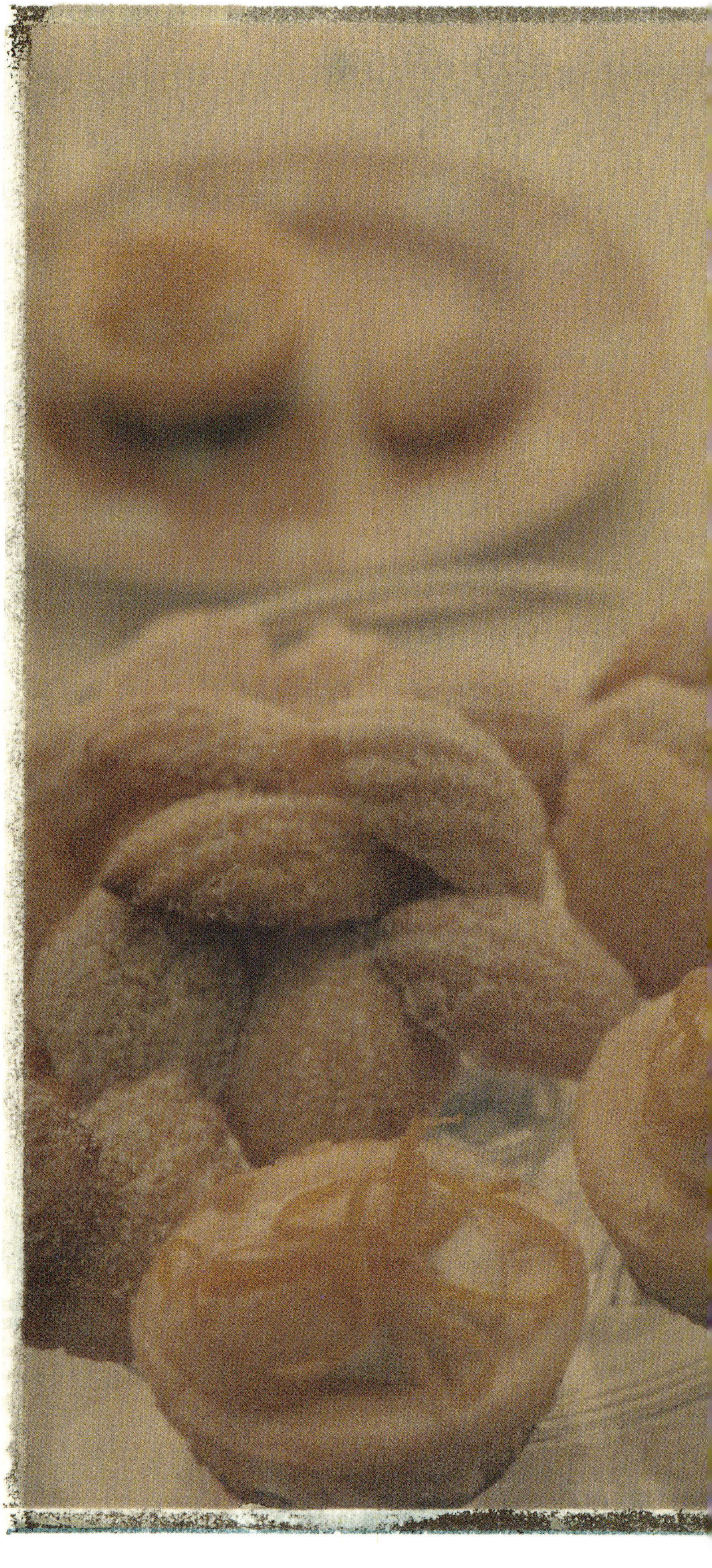

Tiny lime and lemon madelines. Lemon curd cheesecakes.

LEMON CURD CHEESECAKES

INGREDIENTS

Base

½ cup (60 g/2 oz) plain sweet biscuit (cookie) crumbs

½ cup (50 g/2 oz) ground almonds

60 g (2 oz) butter, melted

Topping

¾ cup (185 g/6 oz) cream cheese, chopped

⅓ cup (90 g/3 oz) sour cream

2 tablespoons lemon juice

3 tablespoons caster (superfine) sugar

1 egg

½ teaspoon vanilla extract

To Serve

½ quantity lemon curd (page 168)

More tiny tea party treats.

Place the biscuit crumbs, ground almonds and butter in a bowl and mix to combine. Press the mixture firmly into the bases of twelve 6 cm (2½ in) round patty tins (muffin pans) and set aside.

To make topping, place cream cheese, sour cream, lemon juice, caster sugar, egg and vanilla in a bowl and beat well until smooth. Divide the topping between the patty tins and bake in a preheated oven at 180°C (355°F) for 15 minutes or until firm. Allow to cool in the tins before removing gently with a knife.

To serve, top the cheesecakes with lemon curd and candied lemon peel with a small spoonful of heavy (double) cream on the side.

MAKES 12

LITTLE LEMON PUDDINGS

INGREDIENTS

125 g (4 oz) butter

1½ cups (250 g/8 oz) demerara sugar

2 tablespoons grated lemon rind

½ cup (125 mL/4 fl oz) lemon juice

4 eggs, separated

¾ cup (90 g/3 oz) self-raising flour

½ cup (125 mL/4 fl oz) milk

icing (confectioners') sugar for dusting

Perfect winter comfort food.

Place the butter, sugar and lemon rind in a bowl and beat until light and creamy. Gradually add the lemon juice and egg yolks and beat well. Fold the flour and milk through the mixture. In a separate bowl, beat the egg whites until soft peaks form and fold them through the mixture. Pour into eight greased 1 cup (250 mL/8 fl oz) capacity ramekins or tea cups.

Put the ramekins in a baking pan and add enough hot water to come half way up the sides of the ramekins. Bake in a preheated oven at 180°C (355°F) for 20 minutes or until the puddings are puffed and golden. The puddings should be soft and saucy in the bottoms. Dust with icing sugar before serving. Serve immediately with a side ramekin of vanilla bean ice cream.

SERVES 8

LIME AND COCONUT SYRUP CAKE

Place the butter, rind and sugar in a bowl and beat until light and creamy. Gradually add the eggs and beat well. Fold through the coconut and flour and pour the mixture into a greased 20 cm (8 in) round cake tin. Bake in a preheated oven at 160°C (315°F) for 45 minutes or until the cake is cooked when tested with a skewer.

To make lime syrup, place the ingredients in a saucepan over a low heat. Stir until the sugar has completely dissolved. Increase the heat and simmer the syrup for 4 minutes. Remove the rind and set aside. Pour the hot syrup over the hot cake in the tin and stand for 2 minutes before removing the cake from the tin.

To serve, decorate the cake with candied rind and serve with any extra syrup and heavy (double) cream.

SERVES 8

INGREDIENTS

125 g (4 oz) butter

2 teaspoons grated lime rind

1 cup (225 g/7 oz) caster (superfine) sugar

4 eggs

2 cups (185 g/6 oz) desiccated coconut

1 cup (125 g/4 oz) self-raising flour

Lime Syrup

1 cup (250 g/8 oz) white granulated sugar

2 tablespoons lime juice

3/4 cup (185 mL/6 fl oz) water

strips of rind from 1 lime

TUNA AND WASABI MAYO SANDWICHES

Delicate tuna and oyster mushrooms with a creamy wasabi kick—superb.

Heat the oils in a frying pan or skillet over a medium heat, add the ginger and sauté for 1 minute. Add the sake, tamari, lime rind and mushrooms and sauté for a further 2–3 minutes or until the mushrooms are soft.

To make wasabi mayonnaise, place the ingredients in a bowl and mix to combine.

To serve, place small piles of the mushroom mixture on the sourdough rounds. Top generously with slices of tuna and drizzle with wasabi mayonnaise. Serve immediatly with drinks or serve a few as a first course.

SERVES 6 FOR DRINKS OR 4 AS A FIRST COURSE

INGREDIENTS

1 teaspoon sesame oil

1 teaspoon vegetable oil

1 tablespoon grated fresh ginger

2 tablespoons sake

2 tablespoons tamari

1 teaspoon grated lime rind

310 g (10 oz) oyster mushrooms

12 small slices sourdough bread, toasted

405 g (13 oz) tuna, thinly sliced

Wasabi Mayonnasie

2 teaspoons wasabi paste

1/3 cup (90 g/3 oz) mayonnaise

1 tablespoon lime juice

1 teaspoon cracked Szechuan pepper

Winterfruits.

CHAPTER 13

Winter fruits

HAZELNUT CAKE WITH PEARS

INGREDIENTS

2 cups (340 g/11 oz) roasted hazelnuts, ground

½ cup (60 g/2 oz) pecan nuts, ground

1⅓ cups (335 g/10½ oz) caster (superfine) sugar

1½ tablespoons grated lemon rind

5 eggs, separated

⅓ cup (45 g/1½ oz) cornflour (cornstarch)

1½ cups (250 g/8 oz) carrots, grated

½ teaspoon ground cinnamon

3 tablespoons lemon juice

2 tablespoons white granulated sugar, extra

Sautéed Pears

2 tablespoons butter

4 pears, cored and quartered

3 tablespoons brandy

2 tablespoons soft brown sugar

1 nutmeg for grating

Place the hazelnuts, pecans, sugar and lemon rind into a large mixing bowl. Place the egg yolks, cornflour, carrots, cinnamon and lemon juice in the bowl of the food processor and process until smooth. Add the carrot mixture to the nut mixture in the mixing bowl.

Beat the egg whites until soft peaks form. Gradually add the extra sugar and beat until glossy. Fold the egg whites through the nut and carrot mixture then pour into a greased and lined 25 cm (10 in) round springform (removable base) cake tin. Bake in a preheated oven at 180°C (355°F) for 1 hour or until the cake is cooked when tested with a skewer. If the cake becomes too brown during cooking loosely cover it with aluminium kitchen foil. Allow the cake to cool in the tin for 15 minutes before removing it to a wire cake cooler.

To make sautéed pears, melt the butter in a frying pan or skillet over a high heat. Add the pears and sauté for 4 minutes or until they are beginning to soften. Add the brandy and brown sugar to the pan and allow to simmer for 2 minutes.

Serve warm hazelnut cake accompanied by a few pieces of sautéed pears and a dollop of heavy cream. Dust with freshly grated nutmeg.

SERVES 8

FREE FORM TART

INGREDIENTS

1 quantity sweet shortcrust pastry (page 168)

1 egg white

Filling

5 apples, peeled

1 cinnamon stick

2 tablespoons white granulated sugar

Roll out the pastry into a roughly round shape on a lightly floured surface until it is 4 mm (⅙ in) thick. Brush away any excess flour and then brush the top surface of the pastry with egg white.

To make filling, cut the apples into quarters and remove the cores. Place the apples in a saucepan and half fill with water. Add the cinnamon stick and bring to the boil. Allow to boil for 4 minutes or until the apples are soft, then drain them well.

Place the apples on the pastry surface which has been brushed with egg white and arrange them from the centre out. Gather extra pastry around the apples and fold it inwards to form a folded rim. Sprinkle the apples with the sugar and place the tart on a greased baking sheet. Place the tart in the freezer for 10 minutes to ensure that the pastry is firm. Bake the tart in a preheated oven at 200°C (390°F) for 30 minutes or until the pastry is golden and crisp. Serve the tart warm, cut into wedges, with scoops of caramel ice cream.

SERVES 6–8

PASSIONFRUIT CAKES, SABAYON

Pour the sponge mixture into a greased 30 cm × 24 cm (12 in × 10 in) and 2 cm (⅔ in) deep Swiss roll tin. Bake in a preheated oven at 180°C (355°F) for 10–12 minutes or until the cake is springy to the touch. Stand in the tin for 4 minutes then remove and cool on a wire rack. When the sponge is cool, cut the cake into eight equal squares. To make filling, place the cream in a bowl and beat until thick. Fold through the icing sugar, passionfruit and lime rind. Generously spread half the sponge squares with the filling and place the remaining squares on top to form a sandwich. Place each sandwich on an individual serving plate and chill until required.

To make sabayon, place the egg yolks and caster sugar in a heatproof bowl and beat until thick and pale. Beat through the marsala and place the bowl over a saucepan of simmering water. Continue to beat for 10 minutes or until the mixture is very thick. Remove the bowl from the heat and continue beating for 5 minutes or until the mixture has cooled. Fold through the passionfruit pulp.

To serve, spoon the sabayon generously over each sponge sandwich and place under a preheated griller (broiler) for 2 minutes or until the sabayon is golden. Serve immediately.

SERVES 4

INGREDIENTS

½ quantity sponge cake mixture (page 169)

Filling

1 cup (250 mL/8 fl oz) heavy (double) cream

1 tablespoon icing (confectioners') sugar

½ cup (125 mL/4 fl oz) passionfruit pulp

2 teaspoons grated lime rind

Sabayon

6 egg yolks

1 tablespoon caster (superfine) sugar

1 cup (250 mL/8 fl oz) marsala

3 tablespoons passionfruit pulp

PERSIMMON TART

Roll out the pastry on a lightly floured surface until it is 4 mm (⅙ in) thick. Place the pastry in a greased 23 cm (9 in) removable base tart tin and trim the edges. Place nonstick baking parchment in the pastry shell, fill with baking weights or rice and place in a preheated oven. Bake at 200°C (390°F) for 10 minutes. Remove the weights and parchment and return to the oven for a further 10 minutes or until the pastry is golden brown.

To make filling, place the egg yolks, sugar, persimmon pulp and lemon rind in a heatproof bowl. Place the bowl over a saucepan of simmering water and stir until the mixture thickens. Remove the bowl from the heat and stir the butter through the mixture, a few pieces at a time. Allow the mixture to cool and then beat the cream and fold it through. Pour the mixture into the pastry shell and refrigerate for 4 hours or until set. To serve, top with slices of persimmon, cut the tart into wedges, and serve with crème fraîche.

SERVES 6–8

INGREDIENTS

1 quantity sweet shortcrust pastry (page 168)

Filling

6 egg yolks

1 cup (250 g/8 oz) white granulated sugar

½ cup (125 mL/4 fl oz) persimmon pulp

1 tablespoon finely grated lemon rind

125 g (4 oz) butter, chopped

1 cup (250 mL/8 fl oz) heavy (double) cream

2 persimmons

PEAR GALETTES

INGREDIENTS

340 g (11 oz) ready-made puff pastry

Topping

1 cup (100 g/3½ oz) ground almonds

1 egg white

1 teaspoon vanilla extract

45 g (1½ oz) butter, melted

3 tablespoons caster (superfine) sugar

3 pears, peeled, cored and sliced

3 tablespoons demerara sugar

mascarpone and soft brown sugar

Roll out the pastry on a lightly floured surface until it is 4 mm (⅙ in) thick. Cut the pastry into six 15 cm × 10 cm (6 in × 4 in) rectangles. Place the pastry rectangles on baking sheets and refrigerate until required.

To make topping, place almonds, egg white, vanilla extract, butter and caster sugar in a bowl and mix to a thick paste. Spread the pastries thickly with the almond mixture and top with slices of pear. Sprinkle with demerara sugar and place in a preheated oven. Bake at 200°C (390°F) for 15 minutes or until the pastry is golden and puffed.

To serve, place the galettes on individual serving plates. Place a spoonful of mascarpone on each plate and sprinkle with brown sugar. Serve with clusters of toffee-coated nuts.

MAKES 6 GALETTES

APPLE BRIOCHE PUDDING

INGREDIENTS

30 g (1 oz) butter

4 apples, peeled and cored

60 g (2 oz) butter, extra

1 cup (155 g/5½ oz) soft brown sugar

3 tablespoons Calvados or brandy

8 slices brioche or panettone

6 eggs, lightly beaten

1 cup (250 mL/8 fl oz) light (single) cream

1 cup (250 mL/8 fl oz) milk

2 teaspoons vanilla extract

1 tablespoon grated orange rind

Melt the butter in a large frying pan or skillet over a medium heat. Slice the apples and add them to the frying pan. Cook for 6 minutes or until the apples are golden brown. Remove the apples from the pan and set them aside.

Add the extra butter to the frying pan with the sugar and Calvados and stir, simmering, until the mixture has thickened and caramelised. Place a layer of apples in the base of a greased 21 cm × 14 cm (9 in × 6 in) loaf pan. Pour half the caramel over the apples. Top with a layer of brioche then apples and a few spoonfuls of caramel. Repeat the layers ending with a layer of brioche. Place the eggs, cream, milk, vanilla extract and orange rind in a bowl and whisk to combine. Pour the egg mixture slowly over the brioche until the pan is full. Stand for 5 minutes. Add any remaining egg mixture as the pudding stands and the mixture soaks into the bread.

Put the loaf pan into a baking pan and three-quarters fill it with cold water. Place the pan in a preheated oven and bake at 180°C (355°F) for 45–55 minutes or until the pudding is firm to the touch. Remove the loaf pan from the baking pan and allow the pudding to stand for 5 minutes before inverting it onto a serving plate.

To serve, cut the pudding into slices and serve them warm with a spoonful of heavy (double) cream.

SERVES 6–8

Pear galettes.

CREME BRULEE WITH SPICED RHUBARB

INGREDIENTS

2 cups (500 mL/16 fl oz) light (single) cream

1 vanilla bean

2 tablespoons white granulated sugar

5 egg yolks

⅓ cup (90 g/3 oz) white granulated sugar, extra

Spiced Rhubarb

4 rhubarb stalks

3 tablespoons water

2 tablespoons soft brown sugar

3 tablespoons red wine

1 clove

1 vanilla bean

1 cinnamon stick

1 nutmeg for grating

This recipe is for Jody, my supportive work colleague and good friend. It is one of her favourite desserts. Jody always insists on serving the fruit separate from the brûlée, but you can mix them if you like.

To make brûlée, place the cream and vanilla bean in a saucepan and bring to the boil over a high heat. Remove from the heat and allow the vanilla bean to infuse into the cream for 10 minutes.

Place the sugar and egg yolks in a bowl and beat until thick and pale then remove the vanilla bean from the cream and stir through. Pour the mixture into six ½ cup (125 mL/4 fl oz) ramekins and place them in a baking pan. Half fill the pan with cold water and bake in a preheated oven at 200°C (390°F) for 15 minutes or until the tops have set (the custard underneath will still be liquid). Remove the ramekins from the baking pan and refrigerate for 4–6 hours or until the brûlées are cold and firm.

Put the ramekins in a baking pan and place ice cubes around them. Sprinkle the top of each custard with the extra sugar and place them under a hot griller (broiler) until the sugar melts and caramelises.

To make spiced rhubarb, chop the rhubarb into long pieces and place it in a saucepan with the water, sugar, wine, clove, vanilla bean and cinnamon stick. Allow the mixture to simmer for 5 minutes or until the rhubarb is just tender. Remove the clove, vanilla bean and cinnamon stick.

To serve, place a crème brûlée on each serving plate. Place a few spoonfuls of spiced rhubarb next to each brûlée and finish with freshly grated nutmeg.

SERVES 6

POMEGRANATE AND MASCARPONE PUDDING

Pour the sponge mixture into a greased 25 cm (10 in) springform (removable base) cake tin and bake in a preheated oven at 180°C (355°F) for 30–35 minutes or until the cake is springy to the touch. Allow the cake to cool on a wire rack and then slice it into four even layers. To make filling, place pomegranate juice, mascarpone, cream and caster sugar in a bowl and beat until light and thick. To make pomegranate syrup, place pomegranate juice, brandy and sugar in a small saucepan and simmer over a low heat until the syrup has reduced by half. To assemble pudding, place a layer of sponge in the base of a lined 25 cm (10 in) springform cake tin. Brush with a quarter of the syrup and top with a quarter of the filling. Repeat the layers, finishing with a layer of the filling. Cover and refrigerate the pudding for at least 3 hours.

To serve, remove the pudding from the tin and sprinkle it with pomegranate seeds and dust with cocoa. Slice into wedges and serve.

SERVES 8–10

INGREDIENTS

1 quantity sponge cake mixture (page 169)

Filling
½ cup (125 mL/4 fl oz) pomegranate juice
2 cups (500 g/1 lb) mascarpone
1½ cups (375 mL/12 fl oz) heavy (double) cream
2 tablespoons caster (superfine) sugar

Pomegranate Syrup
1 cup (250 mL/8 fl oz) pomegranate juice
⅓ cup (90 mL/3 fl oz) brandy
1 tablespoon white granulated sugar

pomegranate seeds
cocoa powder for dusting

QUINCES WITH ANGLAISE

Place the water and sugar in a saucepan and stir over a low heat until the sugar dissolves. Add the quinces and bay leaf, cover and simmer slowly for 4–5 hours or until they are a ruby pink colour. Keep them warm.

To make lemon scented anglaise, place the milk, vanilla bean, lemon rind and sugar in a saucepan over a medium heat and heat until almost boiling. Remove from the heat and whisk through the egg yolks. Combine the cornflour and water and mix until smooth. Whisk it into the anglaise. Return the saucepan to the heat and stir until the mixture thickens slightly. Remove the vanilla bean and lemon rind.

To serve, place spoonfuls of the anglaise on large, individual serving plates, top with two quince halves and decorate with candied lemon peel.

SERVES 4

INGREDIENTS

8 cups (2 litres/3¼ imp. pints) water
¾ cup (185 g/6 oz) white granulated sugar
4 quinces, peeled and halved
1 bay leaf
candied lemon peel

Lemon Scented Anglaise
2 cups (500 mL/16 fl oz) milk
1 vanilla bean
3 pieces lemon rind
2½ tablespoons white granulated sugar
4 egg yolks
2 teaspoons cornflour (cornstarch)
1 tablespoon water

chocolate and coffee.

CHAPTER 14

Chocolate and coffee

RICH ALMOND COFFEE CAKE

INGREDIENTS

1½ cups (250 g/8 oz) blanched almonds

¾ cup (165 g/6 oz) caster (superfine) sugar

125 g (4 oz) butter

1 egg

3 tablespoons strong black coffee

1 teaspoon vanilla extract

1 cup (125 g/4 oz) self-raising flour

½ teaspoon baking powder

Place the almonds on a baking sheet and cook in a preheated oven at 180°C (355°F) for 4 minutes or until golden brown. Place the almonds in a food processor or blender and process until finely ground.

Place the caster sugar and butter in a bowl and beat until light and fluffy. Add the egg and beat well. Fold in the almonds, coffee, vanilla extract, flour and baking powder and mix until all ingredients are combined.

Pour the mixture into a greased 20 cm (8 in) removable base cake tin and bake in a preheated oven at 180°C (355°F) for 45 minutes or until the cake is cooked when tested with a skewer. Let the cake stand in the tin for 10 minutes before turning onto a wire rack to cool.

Serve cut into thin wedges with cream and a cup of espresso.

SERVES 12

MY CHOCOLATE MUD CAKE

INGREDIENTS

310 g (10 oz) dark chocolate, chopped

250 g (8 oz) butter

5 eggs, separated

2 tablespoons white granulated sugar

1 teaspoon vanilla extract

⅓ cup (45 g /1½ oz) self-raising flour

The only thing anybody remembers about my 21st birthday party. I'm not sure whether that's a good or bad thing!

Place the chocolate and butter in a saucepan over a very low heat and stir until melted and smooth. Remove from the heat and set aside to cool slightly.

Put the egg yolks, sugar and vanilla extract in a bowl and beat until pale and thick. Fold the chocolate mixture and flour into the egg yolks. Place the egg whites in a bowl and beat until stiff peaks form. Fold the egg whites into the chocolate mixture.

Pour the mixture into a greased and lined (with baking parchment) 20 cm (8 in) round cake tin and bake in a preheated oven at 120°C (245°F) for 1¼ hours or until the cake is firm to the touch but still fudgy. Allow the cake to cool in the oven.

To serve, remove the cake from the tin and serve it warm or at room temperature with heavy (double) cream and a pile of berries.

SERVES 8

WHITE CHOCOLATE SAUTERNES CAKE

Serve small wedges accompanied by a glass of chilled Sauternes.

Place the butter and sugar in a bowl and beat until light and creamy. Gradually add the eggs and beat well. Stir in the buttermilk and Sauternes. Sift the flours into the mixture and add the chocolate.

Pour into a greased 23 cm (9½ in) fluted ring tin and bake in a preheated oven at 180°C (355°F) for 1 hour or until the cake is cooked when tested with a skewer. Warm the extra Sauternes and pour it over the hot cake. Allow to stand for 5 minutes before removing the cake from the tin and serving.

SERVES 12

INGREDIENTS

250 g (8 oz) butter

1½ cups (375 g/ 12 oz) white granulated sugar

4 eggs

¾ cup (185 mL/ 6 fl oz) buttermilk

¼ cup (60 mL/2 fl oz) Sauternes

1½ cups (185 g/6 oz) plain (all-purpose) flour

1 cup (125 g/4 oz) self-raising flour

250 g (8 oz) white chocolate melted

¼ cup (60 mL/2 fl oz) Sauternes, extra

SIMPLE CHOCOLATE HAZELNUT CAKE

Melt the chocolate and butter in a saucepan over a low heat and stir until smooth. Add the cocoa powder and stir until combined. Place the eggs, sugar and brandy in a bowl and whisk until well combined. Stir through the chocolate mixture and add the hazelnuts.

Pour the mixture into a greased and lined 20 cm (8 in) round cake tin and bake in a preheated oven at 160°C (315°F) for 35 minutes or until cooked when tested with a skewer. Cool in the tin.

To serve, cut into thin wedges and serve with a chocolate fudge sauce and vanilla bean ice cream.

SERVES 8–10

INGREDIENTS

125 g (4 oz) dark chocolate, chopped

125g (4 oz) butter, chopped

½ cup (60 g/2 oz) cocoa powder

3 eggs

¼ cup (60 g/2 oz) white granulated sugar

3 tablespoons brandy

¾ cup (125 g/4 oz) chopped roasted hazelnuts

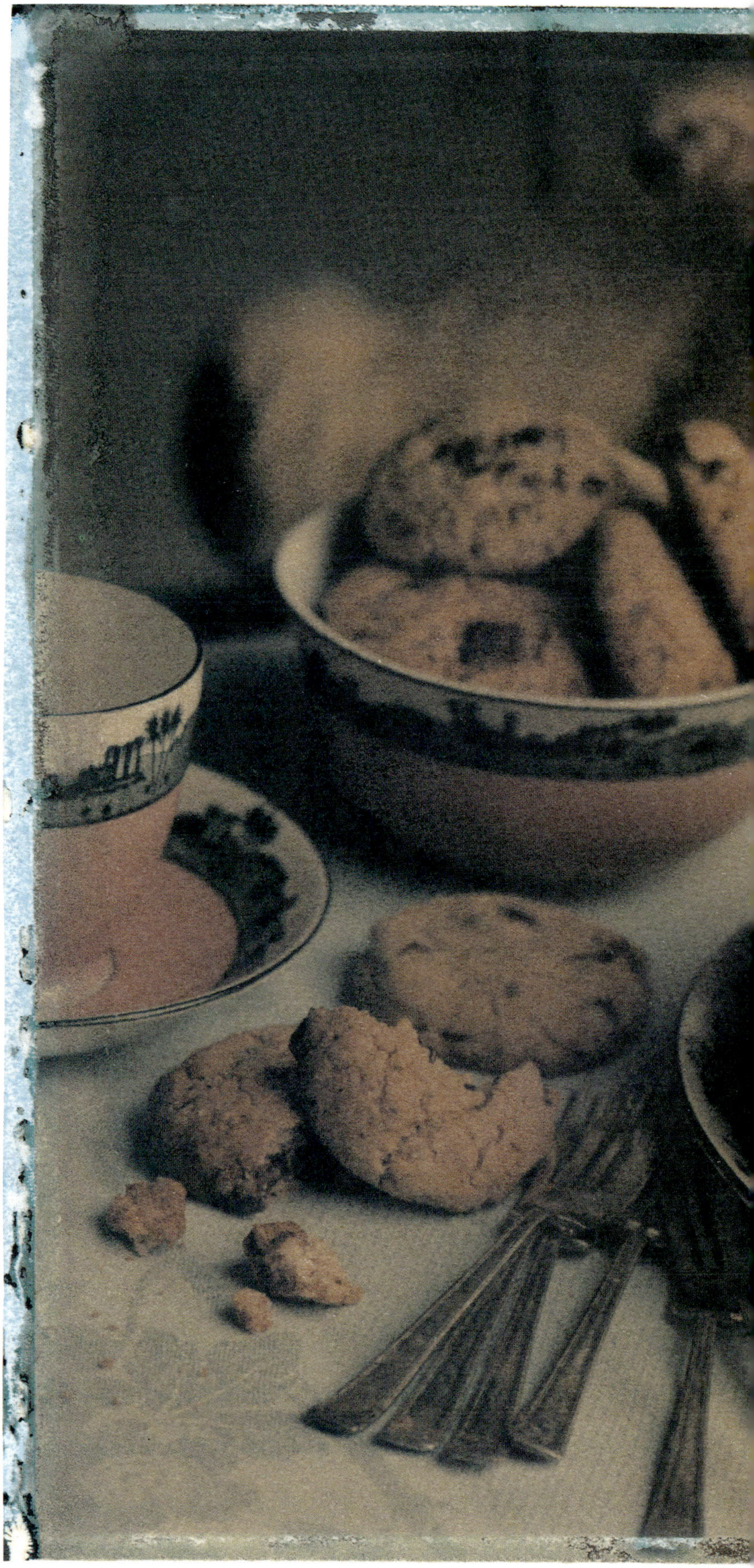

Chocolate cake for a glass of milk and Chocolate chip cookies.

CHOCOLATE CAKE FOR A GLASS OF MILK

INGREDIENTS

185 g (6 oz) butter

1½ cups (340 g/11 oz) caster (superfine) sugar

2 teaspoons vanilla extract

3 eggs

½ cup (125 g/3 oz) sour cream

¾ cup (185 mL/ 6 fl oz) milk

1¼ cups (155 g/ 5 oz) self-raising flour

¾ cup (90 g/3 oz) plain (all-purpose) flour

⅔ cup (75 g/2½ oz) cocoa powder

Chocolate Cream

250 g (8 oz) dark chocolate

125 g (4 oz) butter

3 tablespoons light (single) cream

chocolate curls

You can't have one without the other.

Place the butter, caster sugar and vanilla extract in a bowl and beat until light and fluffy. Gradually add the eggs and beat well. Whisk in the sour cream and milk. Sift together the flours and cocoa powder and fold into the cake mixture. Pour the mixture into a greased 23 cm (9½ in) round cake tin and bake in a preheated oven at 190°C (375°F) for 55 minutes or until cooked when tested with a skewer. Allow the cake to cool on a wire rack.

To make chocolate cream, place the chocolate and butter in a saucepan over a very low heat and stir until smooth. Remove from the heat and stir in the cream. Place the mixture in the refrigerator for 10 minutes to thicken to a spreadable consistency.

To assemble, cut the cake in half horizontally and spread the tops of both cakes with chocolate cream. Place one on top of the other and decorate with chocolate curls. Serve cut into wedges accompanied by a glass of ice cold milk.

SERVES 12

CHOCOLATE CHIP COOKIES

INGREDIENTS

250 g (8 oz) butter

1 cup (155 g/5 oz) soft brown sugar

2 teaspoons vanilla extract

1 egg

1½ cups (185 g/6 oz) self-raising flour

½ cup (60 g/2 oz) plain (all-purpose) flour

¾ cup (45 g/1½ oz) shredded coconut

225 g (7 oz) dark chocolate, chopped

1 cup (170 g/ 5½ oz) roasted hazelnuts, roughly chopped

They solved everybody's problems in 'The Brady Bunch' so it is best that we all keep a jar handy.

Place the butter, sugar and vanilla extract in a bowl and beat until light and fluffy. Add the egg and beat well. Fold in the flours, coconut, chocolate and hazelnuts. Roll 2 tablespoons of mixture into balls and place on lightly greased baking sheets. Flatten the cookies slightly and bake in a preheated oven at 180°C (355°F) for 12–15 minutes or until golden. Cool on wire racks and store in an airtight container.

MAKES 32

MACADAMIA BLONDIES

Place the chocolate and butter in a saucepan over a very low heat and stir until smooth. remove from the heat and set aside to cool slightly. Place the sugar, vanilla extract and eggs in a bowl and beat until thick and fluffy.

Fold into the egg mixture the chocolate mixture, flour, macadamia nuts and extra chopped chocolate. Pour into a greased 20 cm (8 in) square cake tin and bake in a preheated oven at 180°C (355°F) for 30 minutes or until the brownie is firm to the touch. Allow the brownie to cool in the tin.

To serve, cut the brownie into wedges and serve them with caramel sauce and vanilla bean ice cream.

MAKES 12 SQUARES

INGREDIENTS

90 g (3 oz) white chocolate, chopped

90 g (3 oz) butter, chopped

½ cup (125 g/ 4 oz) white granulated sugar

1 teaspoon vanilla extract

2 eggs

½ cup (60 g /2 oz) plain (all-purpose) flour

¾ cup (90 g/3 oz) macadamia nuts, roughly chopped

125 g (4 oz) white chocolate, chopped, extra

CHOCOLATE FUDGE BROWNIES

Gooey, fudgy, chocolate, heaven.

Place the butter, sugar and vanilla extract in a bowl and beat until light and creamy. Add the eggs gradually and beat well. Sift together the flours and cocoa powder and add them to the butter mixture. Mix well. Pour the mixture into a greased 23 cm (9½ in) square cake tin. Bake in a preheated oven at 180°C (355°F) for 30 minutes or until the cake is cooked when tested with a skewer. Allow the cake to cool in the tin.

To make chocolate fudge sauce, place the chocolate, cream and butter in a saucepan over a very low heat and stir until smooth. Stir in the brandy and allow the mixture to cool slightly.

To serve, cut the brownie into pieces, cover with the warm fudge sauce and add a spoonful of vanilla bean ice cream.

MAKES 16 SQUARES

INGREDIENTS

250 g (8 oz) butter

1¼ cups (310 g /10 oz) white granulated sugar

1 teaspoon vanilla extract

4 eggs

1 cup (125 g/4 oz) plain (all-purpose) flour

⅓ cup (45 g /1½ oz) self raising flour

¾ cup (90 g/3 oz) cocoa

Chocolate Fudge Sauce

375 g (12 oz) dark chocolate, chopped

¾ cup (175 mL/ 6 fl oz) cream

60 g (2 oz) butter

1 tablespoon brandy or coffee liqueur

CHOCOLATE NOUGAT

INGREDIENTS

2½ cups (625 g/1¼ lbs) white granulated sugar

1 cup (250 mL/8 fl oz) corn syrup

⅓ cup (125 mL/4 fl oz) honey

125 g (4 oz) dark chocolate, chopped

2 egg whites

½ cup (90 g/3 oz) blanched almonds, toasted

½ cup (90 g/3 oz) roasted hazelnuts

rice paper

icing (confectioners') sugar

cocoa powder

Place the sugar, corn syrup and honey in a saucepan over a medium heat and stir until the mixture is warm. Add the chocolate and stir until it has melted. Increase the heat and allow the mixture to simmer for 8 minutes or until the mixture reaches 140°C (280°F).

Place the egg whites in a bowl and beat until stiff peaks form. While beating, gradually add the sugar mixture in a thin stream. Continue beating until all the sugar mixture has been used and the mixture is very thick. Fold in the almonds and hazelnuts and pour into a 28 cm × 18 cm (11 in × 7 in) cake tin lined with rice paper. Cover the nougat with rice paper and press to flatten. Allow to stand for 6 hours or until set (do not refrigerate).

To serve, dust the nougat with the icing sugar and cocoa powder, cut into squares and serve with vanilla coffee. Store the remaining nougat in an air-tight container.

MAKES 32 SQUARES

INDIVIDUAL CHOCOLATE DESSERT CAKES

INGREDIENTS

185 g (6 oz) dark chocolate, chopped

185 g (6 oz) butter

4 eggs, separated

½ cup (125 g/4 oz) white granulated sugar

1 teaspoon vanilla extract

3 tablespoons almond liqueur

½ cup (60 g/2 oz) ground almonds

3 tablespoons plain (all-purpose) flour

3 tablespoons white granulated sugar, extra

Place the chocolate and butter in a saucepan over a very low heat and stir until both are melted and smooth. Remove from the heat and set aside to cool slightly.

Put the egg yolks and sugar in a bowl and beat until light and creamy. Beat in the vanilla extract and almond liqueur. Fold the chocolate mixture, almonds and flour into the egg yolk mixture.

In another bowl, beat the egg whites until soft peaks form. Gradually add the extra sugar while beating, until the mixture is glossy. Fold the egg whites into the chocolate mixture.

Pour the mixture into six greased 1 cup (250 mL/8 fl oz) capacity ramekins or dariole moulds. Place them on a baking sheet. Bake in a preheated oven at 180°C (355°F) for 15 minutes or until the edges are cooked but the middles are soft. Let them stand in the moulds for 3 minutes before removing and placing them on serving plates. Serve with heavy (double) cream or berry coulis.

SERVES 6

chocolate nougat and chocolate dessert cakes.

ESPRESSO BROWNIES WITH LATTE ICE CREAM

INGREDIENTS

½ cup (125 mL/4 fl oz) crème fraîche or sour cream

⅓ cup (90 ml /3 fl oz) espresso coffee

½ cup (90 g /3 oz) soft brown sugar

1 teaspoon vanilla extract

½ cup (125 mL/ 4 fl oz) oil

375g (12 oz) dark chocolate

4 eggs

½ cup (60 g/ 2 oz) self-raising flour

Latte Ice Cream

1½ cups (375 mL /12 fl oz) light (single) cream

4 egg yolks

⅓ cup (90 g/3 oz) white granulated sugar

3 tablespoons strong espresso coffee

1 tablespoon honey

1 teaspoon vanilla extract

For the more refined brownie connoisseur, chocolate with an espresso fix.

Place the crème fraîche, coffee, sugar and vanilla extract in a bowl and mix to combine. Place the oil and chocolate in a saucepan over a very low heat and stir until smooth. Set aside to cool slightly then stir into the crème fraîche mixture.

Add the eggs and fold the flour into the chocolate mixture. Pour the mixture into a greased and lined (with baking parchment) 23 cm (9½ in) square cake tin and bake in a preheated oven at 180°C (355°F) for 35–45 minutes or until the brownie feels just set. Allow the brownie to cool in the tin.

To make latte ice cream, place the cream in a saucepan and stir over a high heat until almost boiling. Remove from the heat and set aside. Place the egg yolks and sugar in a bowl and beat until light and creamy. Add the cream and whisk well. Place this mixture into a saucepan and stir over a low heat until the mixture is hot and has thickened only slightly, then allow to cool.

Stir the coffee, honey and vanilla extract into the cream mixture and pour into an ice cream maker. Follow the manufacturer's instructions until the ice cream is thick and frozen.

To serve, cut the brownie into pieces and serve with large spoonfuls of latte ice cream.

MAKES 12 SQUARES

SPICED HAZELNUT BISCOTTI

An unusual hint of spice make these biscotti taste absolutely scrumptious.

Place the butter, sugar, eggs, pepper, cinnamon, chilli powder, vanilla extract and lime rind in a bowl and beat until well combined.

Add the flour, baking powder, cocoa powder and hazelnuts and mix to a soft dough. Divide the mixture into two portions and roll them into 15 cm (6 in) long logs. Place the logs on lightly greased baking sheets and brush with the egg white.

Bake in a preheated oven at 175°C (350°F) for 20 minutes or until firm to the touch. Allow to cool for 5 minutes and then cut into thin slices. Place the slices on a baking sheet and bake for a further 10 minutes or until the biscotti are crisp and dry. Serve with your favourite coffee or white chocolate and raspberry ice cream (page 85).

MAKES 32

INGREDIENTS

90 g (3 oz) butter, chopped

1 cup (225 g/7 oz) caster (superfine) sugar

3 eggs, lightly beaten

1 teaspoon cracked black pepper

1 teaspoon ground cinnamon

½ teaspoon chilli powder

2 teaspoons vanilla extract

1 tablespoon lime rind

3 cups (375 g/12 oz) plain (all-purpose) flour

1½ teaspoons baking powder

½ cup (60 g/2 oz) cocoa powder

¾ cup (125 g/4 oz) roasted hazelnuts

1 egg white

CHOCOLATE ICE CREAM

Rich, creamy and very hard to stop at one scoop.

Place the milk, cream and cocoa powder in a saucepan over a high heat and heat until almost boiling. Remove from the heat and set aside. Place the egg yolks and caster sugar in a bowl and beat until thick and creamy. Gradually pour in the cream mixture, whisking well.

Pour the mixture into a saucepan, place over a medium heat and stir until it thickens slightly. Remove from the heat and stir through the chocolate then set aside to cool. Pour the mixture into an ice cream maker and follow the manufacturer's instructions until the ice cream is frozen and thick. Serve with hazelnut shortbreads (page 24) or coconut macaroons.

SERVES 10

INGREDIENTS

2 cups (500 mL/16 fl oz) milk

2 cups (500 mL/ 16 fl oz) light (single) cream

½ cup (60 g/ 2 oz) cocoa powder

10 egg yolks

1 cup (225 g/7 oz) caster (superfine) sugar

155g (5 oz) dark chocolate, melted and cooled

MACCHIATTO BAVAROIS WITH MILK CHOCOLATE ANGLAISE

INGREDIENTS

280 g (9 oz) white chocolate

⅓ cup (90 mL/3 fl oz) strong black coffee

2 teaspoons gelatin

1 tablespoon boiling water

1 cup (250 mL/8 fl oz) heavy (double) cream

Milk Chocolate Anglaise

2 cups (500 mL/16 fl oz) milk

4 egg yolks

⅓ cup (90 g/3 oz) white granulated sugar

½ teaspoon vanilla extract

125g (4 oz) milk chocolate, finely chopped

A smooth, coffee flavoured mousse with a milky chocolate custard.

Place the white chocolate and coffee in a saucepan over a very low heat and stir until smooth. Remove from the heat and allow to cool slightly. Sprinkle the gelatin over the boiling water and stir to dissolve. Place the cream in a bowl and beat until soft peaks form. Fold the chocolate mixture into the cream, and stir in the dissolved gelatin.

Quickly spoon the mixture into six oiled ½ cup (125 mL/4 fl oz) capacity moulds. Place the moulds in the refrigerator and refrigerate for at least 1 hour.

To make milk chocolate anglaise, place the milk in a saucepan over a high heat and heat until almost boiling. Remove from the heat and set aside. Place the egg yolks and sugar in a bowl and beat until light and fluffy. Whisk in the milk and then pour the mixture into a saucepan. Place over a medium heat and stir until the mixture has thickened slightly. Remove from the heat and stir in the vanilla extract and chocolate. Continue stirring until smooth and then cover the anglaise and allow it to cool.

To serve, remove the bavarois from the moulds and place them on serving plates that have been flooded with milk chocolate anglaise.

SERVES 6

Macchiatto bavarois with milk chocolate anglaise.

CHOCOLATE MACAROON TART

INGREDIENTS

Base
2 egg whites
½ cup (125 g/4 oz) white granulated sugar
2 cups (225 g/7 oz) desiccated coconut

Ganache Filling
1¼ cups (310 mL/10 fl oz) light (single) cream
310 g (10 oz) dark chocolate, chopped
white chocolate curls
cocoa powder

A chewy coconut shell with a smooth chocolate filling.

Place the egg whites, sugar and coconut in a bowl and mix well to combine. Press the mixture into a greased 23 cm (9½ in) removable base fluted tart tin. Bake in a preheated oven at 180°C (355°F) for 12–15 minutes or until golden. Allow the base to cool in the tin.

To make ganache filling, place the cream in a saucepan and heat over a high heat until almost boiling. Remove from the heat and stir in the chocolate. Continue stirring until the mixture is smooth. Allow the mixture to cool slightly and then pour it into the macaroon shell and refrigerate until set.

To serve, decorate with white chocolate curls and sprinkle with cocoa powder. Cut into thin wedges to serve and accompany with raspberries.

SERVES 12

ESPRESSO GRANITAS

INGREDIENTS

¾ cup (185 g/6 oz) white granulated sugar
1½ cups (375 mL/12 fl oz) water
2 cups (500 mL/16 fl oz) very strong coffee

Perfect on a hot summer's morning for breakfast or brunch.

Place the sugar and water in a saucepan over a low heat and stir continually until the sugar has dissolved. Increase the heat and bring the mixture to the boil. Allow to simmer rapidly for 3 minutes.

Remove from the heat and stir in the coffee. Pour into a deep metal container then cover and freeze for 1 hour. With a fork, whisk the granita to break down the ice crystals and then return to the freezer for 3 hours.

Before serving, whisk the granita with a fork. Spoon into chilled bowls or glasses and top with a small spoonful of whipped cream if desired.

SERVES 6

CHOCOLATE AND RASPBERRY CREAM CAKE

To make cake, place the butter and caster sugar in a bowl and beat until light and creamy. Add the egg yolks and beat well. Sift the flour and cocoa over the mixture and fold in the milk. Beat the egg whites until stiff peaks form, then fold through the mixture.

Pour the cake mixture into a 23cm (9½ in) springform tin and bake in a preheated oven at 180°C (355°F) for 25–30 minutes or until cooked when tested with a skewer. Place the cake on a wire rack and cool. When cold, slice the cake in half and place one half in the base of a 23 cm (9½ in) springform tin that has been lightly oiled.

To make chocolate cream, melt the chocolate and butter in a saucepan over a low heat and stir until smooth. Set aside to cool. Place the eggs and sugar in a bowl and beat until thick and creamy. Fold the chocolate mixture and the cream through the egg mixture. Sprinkle the gelatin over the boiling water and stir to dissolve. Place over a saucepan of simmering water and stir until clear. Cool slightly and fold into the chocolate cream.

Pour half the chocolate cream over the cake base in the tin and place in the refrigerator to set. Leave the remaining chocolate cream at room temperature.

To make raspberry cream, place the raspberries in a food processor or blender and process until smooth. Pour the raspberry purée into a sieve and stir through into a bowl. Stir the sugar into the raspberry purée and fold through the cream. Sprinkle the gelatin over the boiling water and stir to dissolve. Place over a saucepan of simmering water and stir until clear. Cool slightly and fold through the raspberry mixture.

Pour the raspberry cream over the chocolate cream in the tin and refrigerate for 5 minutes or until firm. Pour the remaining chocolate cream over the raspberry cream and add the remaining cake layer. Cover and refrigerate for 3 hours or until firm.

To serve, remove from the tin and decorate with chocolate curls and extra raspberries.

SERVES 8–10

INGREDIENTS

Chocolate Cake

125 g (4 oz) butter

½ cup (125 g/4 oz) caster (superfine) sugar

2 eggs, separated

1 cup (125 g/4 oz) self-raising flour

2 tablespoons cocoa powder

3 tablespoons milk

Chocolate Cream

310 g (10 oz) dark chocolate

155 g (5 oz) butter

3 eggs

⅓ cup (90 g/3 oz) white granulated sugar

1¾ cups (435 mL/14 fl oz) heavy (double) cream, whipped

1 tablespoon gelatin

3 tablespoons boiling water

Raspberry Cream

340 g (11 oz) raspberries

2 tablespoons white granulated sugar

1¼ cups (310 mL/10 fl oz) heavy (double) cream, whipped

3 teaspoons gelatin

3 tablespoons boiling water

Basics.

CHAPTER 15

The basics

SHORTCRUST PASTRY

INGREDIENTS

2 cups (250 g/8 oz) plain (all-purpose) flour
125 g (4 oz) butter, chopped
iced water

Place the flour and butter in a food processor and process until the mixture resembles fine breadcrumbs. While the motor is running, add drops of iced water until a soft dough forms.

Wrap the dough in plastic wrap (cling film) and refrigerate for 30 minutes before rolling. To stop shrinkage of the dough, refrigerate the dough once it has been rolled and place it in the required tin.

MAKES 1 QUANTITY

SWEET SHORTCRUST PASTRY

INGREDIENTS

2 cups (250 g/8 oz) plain (all-purpose) flour
125 g (4 oz) butter, chopped
2 tablespoons caster (superfine) sugar
iced water

Place the flour, butter and sugar in a food processor and process until the mixture resembles fine breadcrumbs. While motor is running, add drops of iced water until a soft dough forms.

Wrap the dough in plastic wrap (cling film) and refrigerate for 30 minutes before rolling. To stop shrinkage of the dough, refrigerate the dough once it has been rolled and place it in the required tin.

MAKES 1 QUANTITY

LEMON CURD

90 g (3 oz) butter
1 cup (225 g/7 oz) caster (superfine) sugar
½ cup (125 mL/4 fl oz) lemon juice
2 eggs, lightly beaten

Place the butter, caster sugar, lemon juice and eggs in a bowl over a saucepan of simmering water. Stir for 5 minutes or until the mixture thickens. When cool, pour into sterilised jars and seal.

MAKES 1½ CUPS

WHOLE EGG MAYONNAISE

Place the eggs, mustard and lemon juice in a food processor or blender and process until well combined. While the motor is running, add the oil drop by drop and process until all the oil is used and the mayonnaise is thick. Stir in the pepper and store in sterilised jars in the refrigerator for up to 4 months.

MAKES 2 CUPS

INGREDIENTS

5 eggs

1 teaspoon Dijon mustard

1 tablespoon lemon juice

2 cups (500 mL/16 fl oz) vegetable oil

¼ teaspoon white pepper

PESTO

Place the basil leaves, pine nuts, Parmesan cheese and garlic in a food processor or blender and process until finely chopped. Gradually add the oil while the motor is running and process to a thick paste. Store in the refrigerator in sterilised jars for up to 3 weeks.

MAKES 1 CUP

INGREDIENTS

1 cup (45 g/1½ oz) fresh basil leaves

3 tablespoons pine nuts

3 tablespoons grated Parmesan cheese

2 garlic cloves, crushed

⅓ cup (90 mL/3 fl oz) olive oil

SPONGE CAKE

Place the eggs and vanilla extract in a bowl and beat until thick and fluffy. Gradually add the caster sugar and beat well. Sift the flours over the mixture and fold through with the butter. Follow recipe instructions for use.

MAKES 1 QUANTITY

INGREDIENTS

4 eggs

1 teaspoon vanilla extract

⅔ cup (155 g/5 oz) caster (superfine) sugar

4 tablespoons cornflour (cornstarch)

4 tablespoons plain (all-purpose) flour

4 tablespoons self-raising flour

2 tablespoons butter, melted

PASTA

Place the flour on a clean working surface and make a well in the centre. Add the eggs to the well and gradually stir in the flour until a firm dough has formed (all of the flour may not be required).

Divide the dough into six equal portions and roll in a pasta machine until thin. Cut or fill as desired.

Poppyseed Pasta: Add 2–3 tablespoons of poppyseeds to the flour before adding the eggs.

MAKES 1 QUANTITY

INGREDIENTS

2 cups (250 g/8 oz) plain (all-purpose) flour

4 large eggs

PIZZA DOUGH

INGREDIENTS

2 teaspoons active dry yeast

pinch white granulated sugar

⅔ cup (170 mL/5½ fl oz) warm water

2 cups (250 g/8 oz) plain (all-purpose) flour

3 tablespoons olive oil

Place the yeast and sugar in a bowl and pour over the warm water. Mix well to dissolve the yeast and set aside in a warm place until the mixture is foaming.

Place the flour in a bowl and make a well in the centre. Add the oil to the yeast mixture, pour into the flour and mix to a soft dough. Place the dough on a lightly floured surface and knead it for 5 minutes or until it is smooth and elastic.

Place the dough in a lightly greased bowl and cover with a clean tea towel. Place the bowl in a warm place and allow the dough to double in size. Punch the dough and knead it briefly before shaping it into the required shapes.

For a thick crust, shape the pizza dough as required and allow the pizza base to stand on baking sheets for 10 minutes to rise, then top and bake.

For a thin and crisp crust, shape the pizza dough as required and top. Slide pizzas onto a preheated baking sheet or tile and follow the cooking instructions in the recipe.

MAKES 1 QUANTITY

ROASTING CAPSICUMS

Remove the tops from the capsicums (sweet peppers) and then remove the centre and seeds. Cut the capsicum into quarters and flatten the pieces. Place the capsicums under a hot preheated griller (broiler) and grill skin side up for 4 minutes or until the skins are charred and black.

Remove from the griller, place in a plastic bag and seal. This will steam the skins off. Allow to stand for 6 minutes then remove from the bag, peel away the skins and use as required.

Pizza dough.

GLOSSARY

Anglaise. A flavoured custard made of egg yolks, sugar and milk.
Antipasto. An Italian term which literally means 'before the meal' and usually refers to an assortment of foods, such as meats and vegetables.
Aöli. Garlic flavoured mayonnaise originating in France.
Arborio rice. A plump, short-grain rice traditionally used for risotto. The best grows in the Piedmont region of Italy.
Baking parchment. Nonstick cooking paper.
Baking weights. Metal or ceramic weights placed on pastry before baking to ensure an even, solid crust. Rice can be substituted.
Balsamic vinegar. The finest balsamic vinegar comes from Modena, Italy and is made from the Trebbiano grape.
Balti. A spicy cuisine from northern Pakistan.
Bavarois. A sweet dessert made of gelatinised cream.
Bocconcini. Small balls of fresh mozzarella cheese.
Bok choy. A variety of Asian cabbage (*Brassica*); eaten raw in salads or cooked.
Bouquet garni. A bundle of fresh herbs, including parsley, thyme and a bay leaf, tied together and used for flavouring in stocks and soups.
Brioche. A French term referring to a light yeast bread.
Bruschetta. An Italian term for bread rubbed with garlic, toasted, then dressed with olive oil.
Caramelised (onions). Sautéed until golden brown.
Cassia bark (cinnamon). A spice from the bark of a laurel tree. Cassia is a redder brown colour and more strongly flavoured than cinnamon.
Chinese broccoli. A variety of Asian cabbage closely related to European broccoli.
Chocolate curls. Decorative chocolate curls made by slowly cutting a strip from a block of chocolate using a knife or a vegetable peeler. Place the chocolate on a cloth while cutting the strip to prevent it from slipping while you cut.
Coconut. Usually dried coconut is used in the recipes. The smallest pieces are known as desiccated coconut, the next size is shredded and the largest is flaked.
Coconut cream. Not to be confused with the sweetened variety, this is a mixture of 1 part water to 4 parts coconut. Coconut milk is a less rich mixture of equal parts water and coconut flesh.
Cornmeal *see* Polenta.
Coulis. A purée of skinned fresh fruit or vegetables, such as the tomato.
Cous cous. A North African staple food made from semolina.
Cracked black pepper. The quantity is not usually specified, use it to taste.
Cream. Light (single) cream refers to pouring cream; heavy (double) or Australian thickened cream refers to cream that can be more easily whipped or served in a thick dollop.
Crème fraîche. A slightly soured cream common in France. It is now readily available, or can be made at home by mixing heavy (double) cream and buttermilk.
Curry leaves. Available fresh or dried, these small, fragrant leaves are often imported from Sri Lanka and used to flavour soups and curries.
Field mushrooms. Large, flat commercially available mushrooms. Do not pick mushroons in the wild unless you are certain of the variety.
Fish sauce. A salty, fermented fish juice.
Galangal. A root similar in appearance and related to the ginger family, substitute ginger if galangal is unavailable. It is used for flavouring in many Asian dishes.
Galette. A round, flat French cake.
Golden shallots (eschalots). The true French shallot, they look like very small brown onions. See also spring onions (scallions).
Granita. The less-refined Italian version of the French sorbet. The name comes from grano, a kernel of grain, it is an ice with a grainy texture.
Haloumi. A savoury, salty Greek cheese made from ewe's milk.
Hard ball stage. When boiling syrup dropped into cold water forms a hard ball. 120°C (245°F) on a sugar thermometer.
Hoisin sauce. Originating in China, a thick, reddish-brown, sweet and spicy sauce.
Kaffir lime leaves. The leaves of a Southeast Asian lime which are used fresh or dried to flavour curries and soups.
Ketchup manis. A dark, thick, sweet Indonesian soy sauce.
Knead. Working dough to form a smooth, pliable mass; done by hand or machine.
Kumara. A variety of sweet potato with orange skin and pink or cream flesh.
Lavosh bread. A flat crispbread often served with cheese.

Lemon grass. A herb, used fresh or dried, most often associated with Thai cooking, the bulblike base imparts a lemon flavour and fragrance, and a crunchy texture.
Macerate. Soaking food in liquid to impart the liquid's flavour to the food.
Madeleine pan. A French, scallop-shape pan.
Marinate. A seasoned liquid in which foods are soaked. The food takes on the flavour of the liquid and also becomes more tender after marination.
Mirin. Japanese fermented rice wine.
Mizuna. A feathery fine leaf from the Asian cabbage family *(Brassica)*, used in salads and stir-fries.
Niçoise olives. Baby black olives from the south of France.
Oil. Sometimes the type of oil has been specified. If not, the choice is yours. Some prefer a full-flavoured oil, such as an extra virgin olive oil but others may prefer a milder flavour. It is a matter of taste.
Palm sugar. A thick, dark brown sugar made from the sap of certain palm trees. A richly flavoured brown sugar can be used instead. Palm sugar is often used to make jaggery.
Panettone. A spiced festive cake originally baked in the shape of a dove.
Pappardelle. A thick, wide pasta, three times the width of fettuccine.
Pasta wheel. An implement used to cut pasta shapes, such as ravioli.
Polenta/cornmeal. A yellow meal ground from corn or maize. It is first prepared as a thick pudding or porrridge and then used in different ways.
Purée. To blend or mash food until it is smooth.
Ramekin. A small, ovenproof soufflé cup of 1 cup (250 mL/8 fl oz) capacity.
Rice paper. A very thin, edible paper used to encase foods.
Risotto. An Italian rice dish where stock is absorbed into the rice, which, for best results, should be Arborio rice.
Roe. Female fish eggs and milt (spawn) of male fish.
Sabayon. A French dessert made by whisking together egg yolks, white wine and sugar. In Italy it is known as zabaglione.
Saffron threads. The yellow stigma from a crocus. The threads are superior to powdered saffron. They should be crushed or soaked before use.
Sake. Japanese wine made from fermented rice.
Salsa. An accompaniment or sauce made from cooked or fresh food.
Sambal. Sambals are condiments or side dishes, usually served with curries and rice dishes.
Sashimi (tuna). Fresh, raw fish, sliced thinly, popular in Japanese cuisine.
Sauté. To cook food quickly in a little oil or butter in a frying pan or skillet over heat.
Sauternes. Sweet, dessert wine.
Shoyu. A light Japanese soy sauce.
Smoking chips. These are available in a variety of fragrant woods, including hickory.
Soba noodles. Brownish coloured Japanese noodles usually made from buckwheat flour, availabe fresh (occasionally) but more often dried.
Spring onions (scallions). Often mistakenly called shallot, they have a greenish-white bulbous end.
Star anise. An oriental spice, the star-shaped pods are used in cooking for flavouring.
Sterilising. Wash and dry the jars and heat in the oven at 100°C (210°F) for 30 minutes.
Stocks. Chicken, beef and veal stocks are available or you can make your own.
Stracchino cheese. A rustic French cheese made from ewe's, goat's or cow's milk.
Sweet potato *see* Kumara
Tahini. Sesame seed paste.
Tamari. A dark, thick Japanese soy sauce.
Tamarind paste. The strongly flavoured paste is made from the pod of the tamarind tree. It is used to flavour Asian curries and the like.
Tapénade. A thick paste, usually made of black olives, capers and anchovies.
Tomme fraîche. A white, fairly bland Italian cheese which is moist and round. The flavour increases over several days.
Tortilla. Mexican unleavened bread used to wrap food eaten with the fingers.
Wasabi paste. This fiery, Japanese version of horseradish is made from an edible root. It is also available in powered form. The green paste is a common accompaniment to sushi and sashimi.
Wontons. Wonton wrappers are made of thinly rolled egg noodle dough. They can be purchased in general and Asian shops.

INDEX

Page numbers in italic indicate photographs.

aioli with garlic lobster tails and grilled limes 94, *95*
almond, rich coffee cake 152; cake with grilled orange sabayon 135
anglaise mint 19; with quinces 149
antipasto, baked peppers 45
apple brioche pudding 146
apricot, chilli sambal with Thai barbecue pork 12
artichokes, sugar baked with avocado salsa 101
asparagus, char-grilled with balsamic 29, *30-31*; and basil soup 28; with cous cous and warm hummus dressing 29; with poppyseed vinaigrette 32; with prosciutto 28; caramelised with tamarind prawns 32; tempura with Asian mayonnaise 33
aubergine (*see* eggplant)
avocado salsa with sugar baked artichokes 101

balsamic, with char-grilled asparagus 29, *30-31*; peach salad 17; salad 81
basil, and asparagus soup 28; feta and tomato pizzas 121; mayonnaise 113
bavarois, macchiatto with milk chocolate anglaise 162,*163*
beans, chilli black-eyed with cornbread 56; snake with cous cous 101
beef, with rich berry jus 89; and cêpes sausages with mash 109; smoked with baked fennel 104; char-grilled with swede puddings 105; wine and mushroom pies 36
beer battered fish with potato crisps 74, *75*
beet greens with caesar dressing 61
beetroot, Japanese stir-fry 106
berry, rich jus with beef 89; free form galettes 84; frosted with hazelnut meringues 83; sponge with lavender cream *82*, 83
biscotti, spiced hazelnut 161
biscuits, vanilla (*see also* cookies) 81
black-eyed beans with chilli and cornbread 56
blood oranges in sauternes *134*, 135
blueberry, salsa with smoked chichen 80; sour cream muffins 84
bok choy with wasabi salmon and sesame 100
breads, flat with onion and potato 76
brie, blue and celeriac soufflés 100
brioche, apple pudding 146; vanilla with slow simmered plums 22, *23*
broccoli, Chinese with egg noodles 68
broth with cous cous and roast tomatoes 50, *51*
brownies, chocolate fudge 157; espresso with latte ice cream 158, *159*
brûlée, lavender with sugar cookies 128
bruschettas, baked radicchio and haloumi 64; tuna and nectarine 14, *15*
butter, lime and dill 126, *127*; syrup with mandarin cake 136; whipped maple 133; brown purée and parsnip 104; sauce 106

caesar dressing with beet greens 61
cake, almond with grilled orange sabayon 135; rich almond coffee 152; chocolate cream with angel food 85; individual chocolate dessert 158, *159*; simple chocolate hazelnut 153; chocolate for a glass of milk *154-55*, 156; my chocolate mud 152; chocolate, raspberry cream 165; white chocolate sauternes 153; hazelnut with pears 144; lime and coconut syrup 141; mandarin with butter syrup 136; passionfruit, sabayon 145; peach crème fraîche 25; potato, Thai, with lime reef fish 122; rose geranium 129; sage risotto 120; salmon, sorrel cream 121; golden shallot with warm garlic tapénade 90, *91*; sponge 169; crisp sweet potato griddle 105
capsicum, pies, free form roast 45; roasting 170; with rocket and olive pizzettas 57; soup roasted with chilli scones 44
cashew nut dip and eggplant 112
celeriac and blue brie souffles 100
cepes sausages and beef with mash 109
champagne, and melon sorbet 24; mushroom risotto 41
cheddar, smoked, frittata with eggplant puree 112; aged and caramelised leek tarts 108
cheese, blue sabayon grilled with gnocchi 72; blue brie and celeriac soufflés 100; cheddar frittata with eggplant purée 112; aged cheddar and caramelised leek tarts 108; farm, and rocket sandwiches 65; feta, basil and tomato pizzas 121; feta and pumpkin ravioli 106, *107*; goat's pies with prosciutto and potato 76; goat's salad with herb ash 122, *123*; mozzarella, smoked, with baked onion 88; Parmesan soufflé with potato and olive 73; Parmesan and ratatouille tarts 48; pecorino and spinach, warm salad 108; Stilton and cress pastries 68
cheesecakes, lemon curd *138-39*, 140
cherry confit with hazelnut shortbread 24
chicken, green fragrant curry 53; lime and lemon grass 133; Balti with green mango salsa 13; with pawpaw and watermelon salsa 16; rosemary skewers 124; smoked with blueberry salsa 80; smoked herb filled with baby eggplants 125; smoked, and grilled stracchino sandwiches 33
chilli, apricot sambal with Thai barbecue pork 12; black-eyed beans with cornbread 56; coconut dressing with Thai salad 49; jam *46*, 47; and lemon olives 54, *55*; and lime ice cream 57; noodle cakes with tapénade 50, *51*; and pepper oil 48; scones with roasted capsicum soup 44
Chinese broccoli with egg noodles 68
chips, winter vegetable 102, *103*
chocolate, cake for a glass of milk *154-55*, 156; chip cookies *154-55*, 156; cream with angel food cake 85; individual dessert cakes 158, *159*; fudge brownies 157; simple hazelnut cake 153; ice cream 161; macaroon tart 164; milk anglaise with macchiatto bavarois 162; my mud cake 152; nougat 158, *159*; raspberry cream cake 165; and raspberry ice cream 85; white, sauternes cake 153
chutney, mustard seed with eggplant and tomato 52; peach, lemon grass and ginger 13
coconut, chilli dressing with Thai salad 49; ice cream with macerated lychees 20; and lime syrup cake 141; toasted salsa with char-grilled mango 17
coffee, macchiatto bavarois with milk chocolate anglaise 162; espresso brownies with latte ice cream 160; rich almond cake 152; espresso granitas 164; ice cream 158, *159*
confit, cherry with hazelnut shortbread 24
cookies, chocolate chip *154-55*, 156; sugar with lavender brûlée 128
coriander and cucumber salad 69
cornbread with chilli black-eyed beans 56
cos, with coddled egg dressing 60; baby, and marinated tuna 66, *67*
cous cous, with asparagus and warm hummus dressing 29; fried leek with harissa 53; lemon with Moroccan lamb 132; Moroccan 117; with snake beans 101; with roast tomatoes and broth 50
cream (*see also* crème fraîche), chocolate with angel food cake 85; lavender with berry sponge *82*, 83; rose tarts and currants 81; sorrel, salmon cakes 121; sour blueberry muffins 84; iced vodka blood plum 21
crème brûlée with spiced rhubarb 148
crème fraîche, ; peppered with sugar grilled figs 19; peach cake 25
cress and Stilton pastries 68
cucumber and coriander salad 69
currant and rose cream tarts 81
curry, fragrant green chicken 53

dill and lime butter 126, *127*
dip, cashew nut and eggplant 112
dressings (*see also* mayonnaise, vinaigrette), balsamic 29; caesar 61; chilli coconut 49; coddled egg 60; warm 108; warm hummus 29; lemon 64; raspberry *62*, 63

egg, coddled dressing with cos 60; whole mayonnaise 169; noodles with Chinese broccoli 68

INDEX 175

eggplant, parchment baked 113; and cashew nut dip 112; purée with smoked cheddar frittata 112; baby, with smoked herb chicken 125; and pistachio pesto pizzas *114*, 115; ravioli *114*, 115; marinated salad 116; sandwiches 113; slow grilled 117; tomato and mustard seed chutney 52; pancakes, char-grilled veal 116
endive and white fig salad *62*, *63*
espresso, brownies with latte ice cream 160; granitas 164

fennel, baked with smoked beef 104
feta, basil and tomato pizzas 121; and pumpkin ravioli 106, *107*
figs, sugar grilled with peppered crème fraîche 19; white with endive salad *62,63*
fish, beer battered with potato crisps 74,*75*
frittata, smoked cheddar with eggplant purée 112; with pesto and potato 77
fudge brownies, chocolate 157

galettes, free form berry 84; pear 146, *147*
garlic, smothered lamb 92; lobster tails with grilled limes and aioli *94*, 95; and onion risotto 92; roast, and onion soup 93, *94*; roast pappardelle 95; grilled polenta 97; potato purée 74; warm tapénade with golden shallot cakes 90, *91*
ginger, peach and lemon grass chutney 13
gnocchi with grilled blue cheese sabayon 72
goat's cheese, pies with prosciutto and potato 76; salad with herb ash 122, *123*
gooseberries with seared lamb 80
granita, espresso, 164; nectarine 20

haloumi bruschettas and baked radicchio 64
hamburgers with red wine onions 96
harissa with fried leek cous cous 53
hazelnut, meringues with frosted berries 83; spiced biscotti 161; shortbread with cherry confit 24; simple chocolate cake 153; cake with pears 144
herbs (*see* individual herbs)
hollandaise, lime with poached ocean trout 132
hummus dressing with asparagus and cous cous 29

ice cream (*see* also sorbet), chocolate 161; chocolate and raspberry 85; coconut with macerated lychees 20; latte with espresso brownies 160; lime and chilli 57; maple with nectarines 25; rose geranium and mango 21

jam, chilli *46*, 47
Japanese beetroot stir-fry 106
jus, rich berry with beef 89

kumquat panforte 136

lamb, garlic smothered 92; seared, with gooseberries 80; Moroccan, with lemon cous cous 132; spiced with caramelised potatoes 77; with sage and rosemary soufflés 124
lasagne, mushroom 40
lavender cream, with berry sponge *82*, 83; brulée with sugar cookies 128
leek, caramelised and aged cheddar tarts 108; fried cous cous with harissa 53
lemon, and chilli olives 54, *55*; cous cous with Moroccan lamb 132; curd 168; curd cheesecakes *138-39*, 140; dressing with sorrel and salmon 64; and tiny lime madeleines 137, *138-39*; poppyseed muffins 133; little puddings 140; verbena syrup with pancakes 129
lemon grass, and lime chicken 133; peach and ginger chutney 13
lime, and chilli ice cream 57; and coconut syrup cake 141; and dill butter 126, *127*; and lemon madeleines 137, *138-39*; and lemon grass chicken 133; grilled with garlic lobster tails and aioli *94*, 95; reef fish with Thai potato cakes 122; Hollandaise with poached ocean trout 132
lobster tails and garlic with grilled limes and aioli *94*, 95
lychees, macerated with coconut ice cream 20

macadamia blondies 157
macaroon chocolate tart 164
macchiatto bavarois with milk chocolate anglaise 162, *163*
madeleines, tiny lime and lemon 137, *138-39*
mandarin cake with butter syrup 136
mango, green salsa with Baltic chicken 13; char-grilled with toasted coconut salsa 17; and rose geranium ice cream 21; sambal 53
maple, whipped butter 133; ice cream with nectarines 25;
marmalade, sweet onion 89
mascarpone and pomegranate pudding 149
mash with beef and cepes sausages 109
mayonnaise, Asian 33; basil 113; whole egg 169; wasabi 141
melon and champagne sorbet 24
meringues, hazelnut with frosted berries 83
milk, glass of, for a chocolate cake 154-55, 156
mint, anglaise with poached peaches *18*, 19; pesto tart and roast tomato 47
mizuna with peaches and raspberry vinaigrette 60
Moroccan cous cous 117; lamb with lemon cous cous 132
mozzarella smoked, baked onions 88
muffins, blueberry sour cream 84; lemon poppyseed 133
mushroom, lasagne 40; wok, with soba noodles 37; dried, oil 41; and golden onion tart 37, *38-9*; pesto filled 40; field, pizzas 36; champagne risotto 41; oyster, tuna and wasabi mayo sandwiches 141; pies with wine and beef 36
mustard seed chutney with eggplant and tomato 52

nasturtium salad and scallop 63
nectarine, granita 20; with maple ice cream 25; salsa with grilled swordfish 12; and tuna bruschettas 14
niçoise salad with oak leaf 61
noodles, chilli cakes with tapénade 50, *51*; egg, with Chinese broccoli 68; soba, with wok mushrooms 37
nougat, chocolate 158, *159*
nut dip, eggplant and cashew 112

oak leaf salad niçoise 61
ocean trout, poached with lime Hollandaise 132
oil, chilli and pepper 48; dried mushroom 41
olive, lemon and chilli 54, *55*; pizzetas with capsicum and rocket 57; soufflé with potato and Parmesan cheese 73
onion, and golden garlic risotto 92; and roast garlic soup 93, *94*; red wine with hamburgers 96; sweet marmalade 89; baked with smoked mozzarella 88; golden tart and mushroom 37, *38-9*; red, pizzas 97; and potato flat breads 76; caramelised tart 88
orange, sabayon, grilled with almond cake 135; blood in sauternes *134*, 135
oregano and creamy polenta with veal 126, *127*
oysters with salmon roe and pawpaw 14, *15*

pancakes, eggplant, char-grilled veal 116; with lemon verbena syrup 129
panforte, kumquat 136
panini, green tomato 54, *55*
Parmesan cheese, souffle with potato and olive 73; and ratatouille tarts 48
pappardelle, roast garlic 95
parsnip and brown butter purée 104
passionfruit cakes, sabayon 145
pasta, to make 169; with rocket sauce 66
pastries, Stilton and cress 68
pastry, shortcrust 168; sweet shortcrust 168
pawpaw, with oysters and salmon roe 14, *15*; and watermelon salsa with chicken 16
peach, lemon grass and ginger chutney 13; crème fraîche cake 25; poached with mint anglaise *18*, 19; with mizuna and raspberry vinaigrette 60; balsamic white salad 17
pears, with hazelnut cake 144; galettes 146, *147*
pecorino and spinach, warm salad 108
pepper and chilli oil 48
peppers, baked antipasto 45
persimmon tart 145
pesto 169; eggplant and pistachio pizzas *114*, 115; mint tart and roast tomato 47; filled mushrooms 40; and potato frittata

77; watercress 65
pies, capsicum, free form roast 45; goat's cheese with prosciutto and potato 76; wine, beef and mushroom 36
pistachio, pesto and eggplant pizzas, 115
pizza, basil, feta and tomato 121; dough 170, *171*; eggplant and pistachio pesto *114*, 115; field mushroom 36; red onion 97
pizzettas, olive with capsicum and rocket 57; zucchini 102
plum, blood, iced vodka cream 21; slow simmered with vanilla brioche 22, *23*
polenta, grilled garlic 97; creamy with veal and oregano 126, *127*
pomegranate and mascarpone pudding 149
poppyseed, vinaigrette with asparagus 32; lemon muffins 133
pork, Thai barbecue with apricot chilli sambal 12
potatoes (*see also* sweet potato, gnocchi), crisps with beer battered fish 74, *75*; garlic purée 74; caramelised with spiced lamb racks 77; soufflé with olive and Parmesan cheese 73; and onion flat breads 76; and pesto frittata 77; pies with prosciutto and goat's cheese 76; Thai cakes with lime reef fish 122; salt and rosemary baked 72; braised saffron 73
prawns, tamarind with caramelised asparagus 32
prosciutto, crisp, tied with asparagus 28; pies with potato and goat's cheese 76
puddings, apple brioche 146; little lemon 140; pomegranate and mascarpone 149; swede with char-grilled beef 105
pumpkin and feta ravioli 106, *107*
puree, of eggplant with smoked cheddar frittata 112; of garlic and potato 74; of parsnip and brown butter 104

quinces with anglaise 149

radicchio baked and haloumi bruschettas 64
raspberry, and chocolate ice cream 85; cream cake 165; dressing *62*, *63*; vinaigrette with mizuna and peaches 60
ratatouille and Parmesan cheese tarts 48
ravioli, eggplant *114*, 115; pumpkin and feta 106, *107*
reef fish with lime and Thai potato cakes 122
rhubarb, spiced, with crème brûlée 148
risotto, golden garlic and onion 92; champagne mushroom 41; sage cakes 120
rocket with capsicum and olive pizzetas 57; and farm cheese sandwiches 65; sauce with pasta 66
rose geranium, cake 129; cream tarts and currants 81; and mango ice cream 21
rosemary, chicken skewers 124; and sage soufflés with lamb 124; and salt baked potatoes 72

sabayon, grilled blue cheese with gnocchi 72; grilled orange with almond cake 135; passionfruit cakes 145
saffron braised potatoes 73
sage, with lamb and rosemary soufflés 124; risotto cakes 120
salads, balsamic 81; cucumber and coriander 69; marinated eggplant 116; endive and white fig *62*, *63*; goat's cheese with herb ash 122, *123*; oak leaf niçoise 61; balsamic white peach 17; scallop and nasturtium *62*, *63*; warm spinach and pecorino 108; Thai with chilli coconut dressing 49
salmon, with lemon dressing and sorrel 64; roe with oysters and pawpaw 14, *15*; cakes, sorrel cream 121; with wasabi and sesame bok choy 100
salsa, avocado with sugar baked artichokes 101; blueberry with smoked chicken 80; toasted coconut with char-grilled mango 17; green mango with Balti chicken 13; nectarine with grilled swordfish 12; pawpaw and watermelon with chicken 16
salt and rosemary baked potatoes 72
sambal, apricot chilli with Thai barbecue pork 12; mango 53
sandwiches, eggplant 113; rocket and farm cheese 65; grilled stracchino and smoked chicken 33; tuna, oyster mushrooms and wasabi mayo 141
sauces, butter 106; gooseberry 80; lime Hollandaise 132; rocket 66; yoghurt 105
sausages, cepes and beef with mash 109
sauternes, white chocolate cake 153; blood oranges in *134*, 135
scallions (*see also* spring onions), braised 93; tortilla 96
scallop, and nasturtium salad *62*, *63*; charred skewers 16
scones, chilli with roasted capsicum soup 44
sesame bok choy with wasabi salmon 100
shallot, golden cakes with warm garlic tapénade 90, *91*
shortbread, hazelnut with cherry confit 24
shortcrust pastry 168, sweet 168
smoked, chicken with blueberry salsa 80; chicken with stracchino, 33; mozzarella baked onions 88
snake beans with cous cous 101
snow pea sprouts, sautéed 69
soba noodles with wok mushrooms 37
sorbet, champagne and melon 24
sorrel, cream, salmon cakes 121; and salmon with lemon dressing 64
soufflé, celeriac and blue brie 100; with potato, olive and Parmesan cheese 73; sage and rosemary with lamb 124
soup, basil and asparagus 28; roasted capsicum with chilli scones 44; roast garlic and onion 93, *94*
sour cream blueberry muffins 84
spinach and pecorino, warm salad 108
sponge, berry with lavender cream *82*, *83*; cake 169
spring onions (*see also* scallions), braised 93; tortilla 96
sprouts, sautéed snow pea 69
Stilton pastries and cress 68

stir-fry, Japanese beetroot 106
stracchino, grilled sandwiches with smoked chicken 33
sugar cookies with lavender brûlée 128; burnt, tangelo tart 137
swede puddings with char-grilled beef 105
sweet potato griddle cakes 105
swordfish, grilled with nectarine salsa 12
syrup, butter with mandarin cake 136; lemon verbena with pancakes 129; lime and coconut cake 141; pomegranate 149

tamarind prawns with caramelised asparagus 32
tandoori baked vegetables 49
tangelo tart, burnt sugar 137
tapénade, with chilli noodle cakes 50, *51*; warm garlic with golden shallot cakes 90, *91*
tart, chocolate macaroon 164; free form 144; caramelised leek and aged cheddar 108; mint pesto and roast tomato 47; caramelised onion 88; golden onion and mushroom 37, 38-9; persimmon 145; ratatouille and Parmesan cheese 48; rose cream and currants 81; burnt sugar tangelo 137
tempura, asparagus with Asian mayonnaise 33
Thai, potato cakes with lime reef fish 122; salad with chilli coconut dressing 49
tomato, basil, feta pizzas 121; roast with cous cous and broth 50, *51*; with eggplant and mustard seed chutney 52; roast and mint pesto tart 47; green panini 54, *55*
trout; herb wrapped and barbecued 126, *127*; poached ocean with lime hollandaise 132
tuna, marinated and baby cos 66, *67*; and nectarine bruschettas 14; sandwiches and wasabi mayo 141

vanilla, biscuits 81; brioche with slow simmered plums 22, *23*
veal, char-grilled, eggplant pancakes 116; with oregano and creamy polenta 126, *127*
vegetables, steamed herb with wontons 120; tandoori baked 49; winter, chips 102, *103*
vinaigrette, poppyseed 32; raspberry 60
vodka, iced, blood plum cream 21

wasabi, mayo sandwiches with tuna and oyster mushrooms 141; salmon with sesame bok choy 100
watercress pesto 65
watermelon and pawpaw salsa with chicken 16
wine, beef and mushroom pies 36
winter vegetable chips 102, *103*
wok mushrooms with soba noodles 37
wontons with steamed herb vegetables 120

zucchini pizzettas 102